Dec, 2011

Neal Samon
Eric Brown

Chicago's Classic Restaurants

PAST, PRESENT & FUTURE

BY NEAL SAMORS & ERIC BRONSKY

WITH BOB DAUBER
INTRODUCTION BY PENNY POLLACK

CHICAGO'S BOOKS PRESS

Edited by Neal Samors, Eric Bronsky and
Jennifer Ebeling
Produced by Neal Samors, Eric Bronsky,
and Bob Dauber
Designed by Sam Silvio, Silvio Design, Inc.
Printed in Canada by Friesens Corporation

For more information on this book
as well as authors' other works visit
www.chicagosbooks.com.
Email: NSamors@comcast.net,
ebronsky@aol.com

Front jacket, clockwise from top-left:
Francesca's on Taylor (courtesy of
Scott Harris), Le Petit Gourmet (courtesy of
Chicago History Museum, ICHI-23123),
Everest Dining Room (courtesy of Lettuce
Entertain You Enterprises), Randolph
Street in 1962 (Eric Bronsky Collection)

Back jacket, clockwise from top-left:
The Purple Pig (courtesy of Scott Harris),
Chef Gabino Sotelino and Jovan Trboyevic
(Eric Bronsky Collection), Avec and
Blackbird (Doug Fogelson photo, courtesy
of Restaurant Intelligence Agency),
Chef Louis Szathmary (Web image)

To my wife, Freddi, our daughter, Jennifer,
and her husband, Michael. We have
dined together often in our continuing
search for "classic"Chicago restaurants.
Neal Samors

To Michele, my wife and dining
companion for 25 years.
Eric Bronsky

To my wife, Bunny, who has joined me
on the quest to partake of the ultimate meal.
We'll let you know when it happens.
Bob Dauber

Authors' Notes

Chicago has always been a city of great restaurants and shouldn't take a back seat to any other city in the world. While prior to the early 20th Century, it was best known for its steakhouses, ethnic restaurants, beer joints and neighborhood dining establishments, the city has been home to some incredibly fine eateries that, over time, became known as "classic restaurants." Many of these developed all around the downtown area but also were located in neighborhoods and suburban areas.

Just what sets apart a "classic" restaurant from all others? We tend to equate classic with "classy," which connotes elegant dining with starched white tablecloths, fine silverware, and impeccable service. Actually, several of Chicago's most revered classics are just the opposite—informal or casual.

The reality is that classics do not fit within any one category or stereotype. The only traits these restaurants appear to have in common is that they possess one or more unique or enduring qualities that somehow set them apart from the pack, making them special. Sometimes all it takes for a restaurant to become a "classic" is the personality of a restaurateur, an innovative menu item, or an association with a celebrity or an event. On the other hand, there are some very fine restaurants which, for lack of any particularly unique or enduring characteristic, never quite achieve "classic" status.

Perhaps the late Chicago restaurant critic James Ward summed it up the best: "Each [classic restaurant] is one-of-a-kind, beyond trendiness and the vagaries of taste, and occupies its own space/time niche. And each has a tremendous influence on anything that follows."

This book is not intended to be a restaurant review guide about such classic restaurants, but rather a detailed look at those restaurants over the past 100+ years that stood out as special eating experiences. It is also a combination of interviews with restaurateurs, chefs and, just as importantly, their customers who were excited to share their remembrances of these extraordinary eating establishments. The authors begin in the period before 1920 and look at how dining changed and where the city's residents went to eat on special occasions. For those of us who grew up during World War II and since, the range of great restaurants could begin with such memorable places as the Stockyard Inn, Café Bohemia, Fritzel's, Henrici's, The Berghoff, the Walnut Room at Marshall Field's, Como Inn, Kon-Tiki Ports, Don Roth's Blackhawk, Lawry's The Prime Rib, The Bakery, Jacques, the Cape Cod Room, Armando's, Pizzerias Uno/Due, George Diamond's, Eli's The Place for Steak, Morton's, Ashkenaz, and the Empire Room, just to name a few.

In doing the research on this book it became apparent that Chicago dining went through a dramatic shift in the early 1970s with the advent of restaurants owned by great restaurateurs like Richard Melman and Larry Levy, who revolutionized dining in Chicago. Beginning with R.J. Grunts and D.B. Kaplan's, they turned eating out into a fun and creative experience. They created a series of restaurants since that time which now dominate the Chicago restaurant scene. Subsequently, other creative restaurant people followed, such as chef/owner/partners Charlie Trotter, Gordon Sinclair, Tony Mantuano, Jean Joho, Scott Harris, Rick Bayless, Paul Kahan and Donnie Madia, Rob Katz and Kevin Boehm, Steve Lombardo and Hugo Ralli, Mary Jo Gennaro, Jackie Shen, and Grant Achatz.

The authors ended up focusing on restaurants in the central parts of the city and nearby neighborhoods. However, we did not wish to deliberately exclude an untold number of neighborhood and suburban places equally deserving of "classic" status such as Black Angus, Jimmy's Place, Pekin House, Sabatino's, The Branding Iron, and Del Rhea's Basket, just to name a few. Yet, if we kept expanding our list of such restaurants the book could become twice as long, so we reluctantly placed a limit on the possible dining establishments to be included in this publication.

In reading this book you will learn much about what the authors consider to be the classic Chicago restaurants of the past, present and future. The majority of these establishments have also become iconic with the city, so much so, that the mere mention of their names immediately conjures up the word "Chicago!" While you may disagree with the designation of "classic" being applied to some of the restaurants described in this book, it is the authors' goal is to stimulate ongoing discussion about the topic.

Acknowledgments

The idea for this book was first conceived by the co-authors Neal Samors and Eric Bronsky a few years ago because we considered it an excellent topic for another of our Chicago books. Then, early in 2011, Robert Adamowski, son of the late Cook County State's Attorney, Benjamin Adamowski, suggested to us that a book on Chicago's great restaurants would be a wonderful topic. We agreed with his suggestion.

We want to express our special thanks to Richard Melman for his continuing encouragement and support for the book that has included, among other things, access to his personal photo and memorabilia collection along with many hours spent being interviewed for inclusion in the book. Several other individuals and organizations took the time to provide photos, menus, and other items from their collections, including Gordon Sinclair, Karen and Tony Barone, Gary Johnson and Allison Eisendrath with the Chicago History Museum, Lawrence Levy, Lawrence Okrent, Rob Gardner Peterson-Krambles Archive, the Restaurant Intelligence Agency, Herb Russel, and Marc Schulman.

The authors wish to also gratefully acknowledge the contributions of the following individuals to the creation of this book. It was our pleasure to interview a wide range of Chicago's contemporary top restaurateurs, restaurant critics, entrepreneurs and chef/owners including: Lawrence Levy, Penny Pollack, Kevin Brown, Gordon Sinclair, Dick Portillo, Phil Vettel, Grant DePorter, Steve Lombardo, Hugo Ralli, Rob Katz, Kevin Boehm, RJ Melman, Jerrod Melman, Donnie Madia, Chef Scott Harris, Chef Tony Mantuano, Chef Grant Achatz, Chef Paul Kahan, Chef Jean Joho, Chef Mary Jo Gennaro, Chef Jackie Shen, and Chef Rick Bayless. In addition, key interviews were conducted with Gary Johnson, Chicago History Museum, Mark Schulman, Eli's Cheesecake and son of the late Eli Schulman, and Janet Davies, ABC-7, WLS-TV.

In addition, the following individuals participated in the development of the book by agreeing to be interviewees and remembering their many experiences at Chicago's outstanding selection of restaurants over the past years. They include: Arnie Weisberg, Barbara Doctor, Betty Schaffel, Bob Bizar, Bob Darling, Bob Kregas, Bob Kryzak, Bob Rubin, Sandy Honer, Bunny Dauber, Carol Marker, Dan O'Day, Dick Kuhlman, Ed Schultz, Gail Gordon, Herb Russel, Howard Altman, Joe Mantegna, Judy Robins, Mike Zissman, Phil Paschke, Phil Shapiro, Sheila Schlaggar, Sue Leiser, and Susan Herman.

And, finally, special acknowledgements must be given to Sam Silvio for another outstanding book design, and to Jennifer Ebeling for her excellent editing of the text of the book.

I have always thought of classic restaurants as big, beautiful, gracious dining establishments that served high quality food in a hushed and welcoming atmosphere at tables with white tablecloths. I would have to admit that my definition of classic restaurants is probably influenced by the fact I am a child of the '40s and '50s who first ate at fine dining establishments in the 1960s.

Chicago is clearly a quintessential American city with restaurants that have always offered diners very straightforward food such as steaks, chops, and fish. It isn't that we don't have fabulous restaurants today, but the whole landscape and genre has changed in a very visceral way. To me, classic means gracious, and I am not sure that we can get gracious anymore without spending a lot of money to dine out. I can remember that when I grew up, the Cape Cod Room in the Drake Hotel was considered to be a classic restaurant, and although it still exists today, my perception is that it has become a place for an older generation.

I have difficulty classifying today's restaurants as classic, based on my definition of the term. I would have to admit that I am more constrained to use the word "classic" because I am inclined to describe contemporary restaurants, which would include those established since the 1970s, using a different terminology. For example, Alinea, one of the best restaurants in the country today, should be applauded, revered, and respected, but I would argue that it is more of a food "show" than a classic restaurant. And, because of the cost of eating at elite Chicago dining establishments, it seems that if you have been there once, you might not be persuaded to eat there again.

I believe that people go out to dinner to relax and have a good time. But somewhere along the line, a few of these very high society places added the requirement that dining should be an educational experience. In fact, at some of our top dining establishments, eating out has become too complicated and not as relaxing as it should be and could be viewed in the same vein as going to the theater.

A key to being a top restaurant in Chicago is that you can have the finest food in the world but if the diner doesn't have a good time or feel welcome, they are not going back. I would argue that even if a restaurant serves just mediocre food that is straightforward, nothing special, and just a teeny notch above what you could have made at home, if you had a fabulous time, you are likely to return. That is especially true if on your second visit, the owner or the manager or your waiter or waitress recognizes you, greets you, and schmoozes you. Then you believe that you are in the sacred territory of being a regular, and you are going back. So, the diner lives up to how they are treated, and usually becomes a regular because he or she is treated right. And being a classic restaurant has a lot to do with attitude and the fact that you are not being rushed through dinner or expected to help clear the table.

Dining in Chicago began to go through a radical change in the early 1970s when restaurateurs Richard Melman and Larry Levy brought a new vigor and updated perspective to eating out. Their view was that just going out for dinner didn't mean you had to be serious in your dining selections. Instead, the diner should sit back and relax and not be challenged by the menu or the environment, and the restaurateur sought to create an entire tableau to transform you somewhere else in the world. In the past, our parents would eat at fancy restaurants that primarily served steak, potatoes in foil, and tomato juice, because, at that time, people went out for a night on the town. They were very straightforward, and you knew what to expect with your multi-course meal, even though you were there for no longer than an hour and a half. Then people like Charlie Trotter, Melman, and Levy changed the landscape, and presented their food in very different ways. Entertainment became the central fixture of the dining experience.

Classic restaurants were where Chicagoans went on special occasions, but they knew what to expect. Yet, Melman brought an element of surprise and fun, and his strength was that he didn't just say "I'm going to have an Italian restaurant or a French restaurant or a tapas restaurant." He did the work...he researched it, he traveled, he developed a team. And then he put a bit of theatricality on it. I think that Rich thought all this through, what he knew his audience wanted.

As for Levy's style, he put his early focus on Spiaggia, which has definitely become the city's classic Italian restaurant, just like Larry and Tony Mantuano make the argument. And, in terms of talent and menu selection, I would also concur that it is, in addition, a gracious place with a fantastic location and view of Michigan Avenue and the lake. Mantuano, who is a chef/partner, made Spiaggia his "baby." He also promotes from within, especially those members of his staff who are definitely committed to continuing his tradition of offering top quality Italian food, which means that he is an old school mentor who is proud of the people who come out of his kitchen.

Then there is the great Charlie Trotter who brought a new elegance and way of looking at food, along with the idea of bringing to the diner ingredients they had never experienced. He continues plating the food "as pretty as a picture" with a "wow" factor. I think that Trotter is the forgotten man, and both diners and restaurateurs owe a lot to him.

If you went out to dinner in 1960, it was because you could afford to do it and had expectations about the variety of foods you were going to be served. However, in contemporary dining, there is the newly accepted use of the word "foodie" that was popularized by such shows as *Top Chef*. The media has turned chefs into rock stars in a media-saturated world. Should we care about the chef's personal life or history or where he went to school? I can remember that we had a good time at The Bakery because we thought that it was an amazing, original experience and we didn't need Chef Louis Szathmary to be on the cover of *People* magazine to enjoy his restaurant. I wonder if things haven't also changed so that there isn't the continuing loyalty to restaurants that there used to be when there was an attachment to the place and the consistency of seeing the same people was an acceptable idea. In those years, we liked restaurants where we knew what to expect.

Today, I continue to applaud creativity, originality, and pushing the envelope because it is exciting and I am the first one to order the most unusual dish on the menu. But, when I fall in love with that specific dish and I go back there and it is no longer on the menu because they are pushing, pushing, pushing for newer dishes and seasonality, I am disappointed. Restaurants don't allow you the luxury anymore of having the menu you may have experienced 20–30 years ago. I think that "you can go home again" in the right circumstance and that you can relive a meal…but they don't let you. Restaurants today would be better served if they kept those entrees on the menu while playing with their specials. So, I simply say to Chicago's restaurateurs: "Please give me a reason to come back, to touch base with you, and not just to see your latest brainstorms."

In our contemporary society, restaurateurs are building empires and that is their business focus. In my mind, they are all standing on McDonald's shoulders in their expansion, and even if it isn't franchising because they keep control, it is the "malling" of America in the restaurant world. There is a whole segment of Americans who, when they are travelling across the country, pull into town and see a type of restaurant with which they are familiar and it makes them feel comfortable. I want to go into a small town, or a big city, and eat someplace that I can't find anywhere else. I would argue that we seem to be losing our creativity in dining. Those types of chain restaurants are popular and crowd pleasers and they are appealing to a different generation but are twisting in the wind to see what people want, and I hope that they are true to themselves.

Do we have classic restaurants today? We might, and Spiaggia might be one of them. Jean Joho's Everest might be a classic, but I would argue that the true test of a classic is also time. So we should review Chicago restaurants again in 10 or 20 years and decide which of today's restaurants pass the test and see if they made it over the long haul.

Café Spiaggia
(courtesy of Lawrence Levy).

St. Regis Hotel coffee shop (courtesy of Gordon Sinclair).

Some Favorite Early Classics

AND ALMOST-CLASSICS

In and Around Downtown

In early 2006, word of imminent changes at The Berghoff Restaurant (1898–present) drew unprecedented crowds to the historic German eatery. Happily, the closure was brief and the family-owned restaurant continues to delight customers with its old-world décor and food with a modern twist (Eric Bronsky photo).

Marshall Field's (now Macy's) legendary Walnut Room, 1907–present (Eric Bronsky photo).

Gary Johnson, President, Chicago History Museum: The Berghoff was legendary for me, but I realize now that I didn't actually visit The Berghoff until I spent my first summer working in the Loop in 1970. That was when I was on the staff of Adlai Stevenson's first campaign for a U.S. Senate seat. We were in an old building on the second floor above Hinky Dink's Bar at 20 N. Clark Street. Just down the street past where they were finishing constructing the First National Bank building, and then east on Adams, was The Berghoff. I remember going there on a few very special occasions during that summer. A part of my heritage is German, and my grandparents would tell me about Chicago when they grew up. Over the years, many people in the neighborhoods still spoke German and they were always going to picnic groves to have drinks and eat German food. The Berghoff was that kind of setting right in the Loop, and when you ate there you felt that you were on a little vacation and kind of ensconced in German Chicago.

Gary Johnson: I have to say that the Walnut Room at Marshall Field's was another classic restaurant, and I associate that place with one of my grandmothers. As a kid, the important part of my visits to downtown Chicago was to go to Marshall Field's. I remember that my grandma Evelyn once told my sister and me before we went there, "You will see Santa Clauses all over the Loop, but the real one is at Marshall Field's." The reward for waiting in line for Santa Claus, and for good behavior in Marshall Field's in general, whether or not it was the holiday season, was that we got to go to the Walnut Room and be sort of a grown up kid in a more civilized environment.

Betty Schaffel, Buffalo Grove, IL: The Walnut Room was a very special place where you would go for lunch with your mom or grandmother—the ladies all wore hats. A big attraction was Field's Special Sandwich. It was a salad—mostly it was a slice of iceberg lettuce on a piece of bread with turkey, bacon, olives, and everything good, and they would cover it with Thousand Island dressing. The other thing I remember was the wait staff—women who had been there for a hundred years. They would wear uniforms and caps kind of like those worn by French maids.

Gail Gordon, Venice, CA: The Walnut Room was a big deal and the place to go before Christmas and Easter. They had the Great Tree at Christmas and the Easter Bunny. They had a children's menu that featured these wonderful little chicken croquettes, and they had little placemats with puzzles on them. So that was like the big event—to go to the Walnut Room when going downtown to shop with my mom. I remember going there as far back as when Marshall Field's had a playroom where you could leave your kids while you shopped.

Hidden on the lower level of Michigan Avenue, Billy Goat Tavern (1934–present) would hardly seem to warrant description as a classic—or classy—eatery. But an intriguing anecdote about its past, and later a television comedy show, instilled fame; it's now one of Chicago's must-see destinations (Eric Bronsky photo).

Italian Village, 1927–present (Eric Bronsky photo).

Miller's Pub opened in 1935 and moved to its present Wabash Avenue location in 1989 (Eric Bronsky photo).

Carol Marker, Gurnee, IL: The Italian Village—very authentic, like you were in Italy. It was 1960 and you felt like you walked into a different country. The service was good, and everyone was very friendly. And even though you felt it was upscale, it was very affordable. They did their best not to charge Loop prices. The wonderful thing about Chicago is that you can take the train downtown—and this is 2011—the Italian Village is still the same as it was in the '60s. It looks the same. It feels the same. It's real Chicago nostalgia.

Phil Paschke, Lewisville, TX: Years ago, I was business manager and controller for the Chicago Lyric Opera. The Italian Village was home to all of the opera singers. Everyone who came to Chicago to perform would go there. As I recall, in 1973 or '74, the fourth Giuseppe Verdi Congress was held in Chicago and they had all of these opera impresarios from around the world, heads of opera companies, composers and so forth. And the Italian Village was kind of the unofficial gathering place. One time we had a big event and the Ambassador from Italy was there. I also remember Maria Callas ate there a couple of times, and so did Pavarotti and Giuseppe Di Stefano. They really loved the Italian Village, and the Village, in turn, catered to them.

Carol Marker: Miller's Pub has been there forever and when you walk in, you feel as though you are in the 1920s. If you like lamb, their lamb sandwich is wonderful. If you want burgers, go somewhere else. Miller's has 40 or 50 different imported beers. It's just Old World Chicago. One of the great things about Chicago is that you can go home again, and that's the feeling you get when you go back to these old, established restaurants.

Kevin J. Brown, President and Chief Executive Officer, Lettuce Entertain You Enterprises: Billy Goat has to be included in a discussion about Chicago classic restaurants because anytime you walk into the bowels of the city you should experience its wonderfully gritty atmosphere.

Dan O'Day, Gurnee, IL: I used to eat at the Billy Goat Tavern at least a couple of times a week. I am a big Chicago White Sox fan and one time when I went in there, Bill Veeck, then the owner of the team, was sitting at the bar with his wife, Mary Frances. I walked up to him and I said, "Mr. Veeck, I want you to meet the Number One White Sox fan at the *Chicago Sun-Times*." So, we bought each other a couple of beers and we talked baseball. You know, he had a wooden leg and back in those days, everybody still smoked. He would take out a cigarette, put his wooden leg up on the stool next to him and strike a wooden match on his wooden leg! He was always quite the showman. It was a once in a lifetime experience for me and the kind of thing that would happen at the Billy Goat.

Ed Schultz, Evanston, IL: I had some wonderful times at the Billy Goat Tavern long before John Belushi made it famous. A lot of people think that the "Cheeseburger, cheeseburger" routine was a Saturday Night Live creation and don't realize that the sketch was based on a real live place. It's also the source of the famous curse placed on the Chicago Cubs by the owner of the Billy Goat, William "Billy Goat" Sianis, when he brought his goat to Wrigley Field for the 1945 World Series and was asked to leave because fans found the smell of the goat to be offensive. In essence, he said the Cubs would never be in another World Series. So far, they haven't.

Herb Russel, Las Vegas, NV: I worked at 500 N. Michigan and right down the stairs from there was the Billy Goat Tavern. I had lunch there occasionally and we'd run into people like Mike Royko and Gene Siskel, as well as other notable Chicago newspaper people. You know, when Saturday Night Live started doing their "Cheeseburger, cheeseburger" routine, the guys behind the counter started hamming it up and it was a lot of fun. And guys who were real smart-asses would go in there and say "We want a Coke," and the reply was "No Coke, just Pepsi."

Barbara Doctor, Arlington Heights, IL: My husband was in sales and did a lot of entertaining of clients and we would go to Barney's Market Club. It was a guy's bar with great food and it was clean. Their catchphrase was "Yes sir, Senator." This was because the owner couldn't remember anyone's name, so he called everybody "Senator." It had this long bar made of dark wood, well-polished, and they had pictures of semi-nude women, which was shocking at the time. My husband would warn me that I wasn't to order any frou-frou drinks like Banana Banshees—I was to drink like one of the guys. I think that's when I developed an affinity for vodka gimlets, and they made darned good ones there.

Sandy Honer, Bartlett, IL: Many years ago when I was still married, my husband and I were celebrating our 10th wedding anniversary and my sister had bought tickets for us at the Boulevard Room at the Stevens Hotel, which is now a Hilton. In addition to it being an excellent restaurant, the big attraction there was an ice show that took place right next to your table! I remember we didn't have to leave to see the ice show. The floor opened up and there was an ice surface there for the skaters to put on their show. Can you imagine what a unique thing that was to have an ice show going on right next to where you were eating?

Haymarket Pub & Brewery, which now occupies the building where the venerable Barney's Market Club used to be, is vying to become a Chicago classic (Eric Bronsky photo).

The Boulevard Room in the Stevens (later Conrad Hilton) Hotel and the Terrace Garden in the Morrison Hotel once entertained diners with spectacular live ice shows (Eric Bronsky Collection).

Jimmy Wong's two restaurants were located downtown and on the North Side. This photo shows the bar at the downtown restaurant (Eric Bronsky Collection).

Herb Russel: Jimmy Wong's downtown—my associate and I would go to Wong's for lunch about every three weeks and we would have Combination #2. My friend would always have a vodka martini with three olives before lunch. Of course, as soon as we would walk in, the waiter would see us and immediately bark out to the bartender, "Hey! Vodka martini dry with three olives," and our meal would be off and running. The food was always very good, and what was neat about the place was a mix of old Chicago and a bit of Chinatown. The décor had numerous pictures on the wall of Hollywood movie stars and other famous people, all with their arms around Jimmy Wong. We never did see any celebrities there because by the time we were regulars, I think the celebrity draw had pretty much dwindled.

Gene & Georgetti (1941-present)
epitomizes old-school Chicago
steakhouses (Eric Bronsky photo).

Joe Mantegna, Los Angeles, CA: Johnny's Prime Steaks was the site of
what became a ritual for Richard Gilliland, the actor, and me when we were
doing *Godspell*. He played Jesus and I played Judas and we shared the
dressing room. On Wednesdays, between the matinee and the evening show,
we would very often go to Johnny's and order the steaks or prime rib. Again,
we were fairly young guys with hair down to our shoulders and we were
basically having the Wednesday Businessman's Lunch along with all these
"suits." We looked very incongruous to their normal clientele because guys
who looked like us shouldn't be able to afford to eat there.

Herb Russel: Riccardo's was just off of Michigan Avenue and was habituated
by lots of newspaper folks—editors, writers, even the press people and ad
agency folks. The place had two levels, and I remember a great mural in the
restaurant. Very good Italian food—great place for lunch. One time, my wife
and I ate there and she had shrimp scampi and the garlic could knock you
out, it was so rich and strong. Another time I remember, the New York-
based president of our company came to Chicago to see the staff and he took
all of us to lunch there. Even he was impressed!

Two competing steak houses, Johnny's and George Diamond, were located opposite each other on South Wabash Avenue (Eric Bronsky Collection).

Phil Stefani's 437 Rush occupies the old Riccardo's space. Inside, Riccardo's original bar remains a gathering place for journalists (Eric Bronsky photo).

Howard Altman, Chicago, IL: I remember on Sundays a friend of mine and I would go to the Corona Café, which was on Grand Avenue and Lower Michigan. The Corona was interesting in that it had a nice dining room with a full wait staff, but in the back of the restaurant was another entrance with a counter for the cabbies, primarily cabbies, so you could go in there and eat virtually the same dinners that were being served in the dining room for a lot less money than you were paying in the dining room. And it was a wonderful place.

A Few Neighborhood Gems

Sheila Schlaggar, Highland Park, IL: "I was around 12 years old, my father took me to a restaurant on Rush Street called Singapore. It was very famous for barbecued ribs. Now my parents kept a kosher home. We didn't have bacon and we didn't have ham, but my father obviously went there and had barbecued ribs. So, when he took me there, it was kind of a secret to introduce me to ribs. And of course, I was not a child to keep secrets and I spilled the beans. My mother was outraged. Then, my father took her to the restaurant and from then on, we had bacon, ham…she got converted and we didn't have a kosher home any more. I don't think the Singapore is there anymore, but that was a wonderful restaurant. It's kind of funny, there were women sitting at the bar and they were unaccompanied. They said, 'Hello,' and they were very friendly and I asked my father, 'Who are those women?' He said, 'Those are B-Girls.' 'What's a B-Girl?' I asked. He said, 'Oh, those are just women who sit at the bar.' Later on, I realized they were hookers and were waiting for prospects."

Sue Leiser, Denver, CO: "The Singapore was my parents' favorite restaurant, and whenever they could or whenever I was around, they would take me there for dinner. I just remember it was wonderful food. And, oh my God, I just remembered…my stepfather, may he rest in peace, loved taking things from restaurants. He would take cocktail forks, he would take iced-tea spoons—it had to be something unusual. Not an ashtray. One day he came home with a coffee pot—you know, like a silver serving piece … not an industrial…well, actually, he took two and I have them here in Denver. He took them from the Singapore. So, for all of the things he took, there was never any accountability, but my mother told me when he took the two coffee pots, he received a bill in the mail. I thought that was kind of funny, and you know what? I don't get rid of anything. I still have them here."

Dan O'Day: "A place for very special occasions was the Marine Dining Room, located in the Edgewater Beach Hotel. It was kind of the jewel of the North Shore. The food was elegant. All of the big bands played there, and I remember they had a nice dance floor. There was even a canvas-covered, wooden plank walkway that led you on to the beach, and that was kind of romantic in those days. If you had your little lady there with you, you'd try to sneak away to get a few kisses and hugs."

In an era when Chicago had a sizable German population, German-American restaurants could be found in neighborhoods throughout the city. Anchoring the old German neighborhood centered on the Lincoln-Belmont-Ashland intersection was Math Igler's Casino, a classic restaurant beloved as much for its singing waiters as its hearty food (Eric Bronsky Collection).

The Edgewater Beach Hotel (1916–1967) contained several restaurants and ballrooms, but its formal dining room, The Marine Room, was a popular destination for generations of North Siders (Eric Bronsky Collection).

24

Phil Shapiro, San Diego, CA: "There was a beautiful restaurant in the Edgewater Beach Hotel—the Marine Dining Room. I remember seeing Eydie Gorme and Steve Lawrence there. When we went, I was still in the Secret Service and had to be very careful about the places we would go. The reason was that if you were spotted at an expensive place like that, the department wondered if you might have been taking bribes; how could you afford to go to a place like the Marine Dining Room; what we were getting paid? In fact, I told my wife that if she saw people that we knew she shouldn't wave them over. Generally we couldn't afford to go to places like that unless it was a gift from my in-laws or they let us use their credit card. But I still recall being terrified that somebody from the Secret Service would see me there and assume that I was 'on the take.'"

Susan Herman, St. Paul, MN: "Sage's East was a wonderful restaurant and they served huge portions. My husband-to-be and I were there on a date and I had eaten my fill. The waiter came to the table and remarked, 'You haven't finished your dinner.' I told him I was full, at which point he said, 'Well, we can't have that,' and he proceeded to pick up my knife and fork, cut up the rest of my dinner, and tried to feed it to me. I did a double-take and said, 'I don't think so.' And he said, 'Oh, c'mon—just a little bit more.' I felt like I was 6 years old all over again. This was a guy who was dressed in the full waiter's black uniform, with the bow tie—the whole bit...and he starts feeding me. I went up to the maitre d' and I said, 'You have a problem," and I proceeded to explain what had taken place. He asked which one was our table. I pointed it out to him, and he said, 'Oh, that's Joseph's table. He does that all the time."

Sheila Schlaggar: I once went to the Imperial House with an aunt and uncle who were visiting from Savannah, Georgia. I recall it was on Walton in the Gold Coast area. I had never been to a restaurant quite like it. We sat down and there were all these pieces of silverware and a very pressed, starched white napkin and white tablecloth. The waiter—not a waitress, but the waiter—gave me the menu, and I was completely overwhelmed by it. I was probably 10 or 11 years old. My parents always made a big deal out of telling this story because I told the waiter, 'I am not accustomed to eating at a restaurant like this.' And of course, my parents and my aunt and uncle laughed, and I didn't know what was so funny. I thought I gave a perfectly mature and reasonable response while I was trying to figure out what in the world I was going to order off of this gigantic menu. It was a beautiful restaurant."

At its height during the '50s and '60s, Rush Street was thick with restaurants, nightclubs, and cabarets. This 1960s menu cover from Mister Kelly's listed the three clubs owned by George Marienthal.

Chicago's neighborhood Italian restaurants have also been extremely popular and include several classics. Como Inn, 1924–1999, was a family-owned 700-seat restaurant and banquet hall on the Near Northwest side (Hedrich-Blessing photo, courtesy of the Chicago History Museum, HB-30810-A).

Barbara Doctor: "The Como Inn had a classic-looking leather and polished wood bar and also had this intimate seating—they were like little coves that were really cozy. It had the aura of the kind of bar that would be frequented by Humphrey Bogart or John Wayne. My boys used to take me there for my birthday, although I would drive and I would pay. My dad purchased a part of the building that housed the Como Inn and moved his business there, so after awhile, it became my favorite place for lunch to go to get a cheeseburger. You wouldn't think so, but they made the most delicious hamburgers there because they were basically grinding up steak for the burgers. What was not to like? Of course, their Italian dishes, like veal parmesan and whitefish al forno, were excellent."

Bob Kryzak, Grapevine, TX: "A special family treat was when my dad would take us to the Como Inn. The meals were magnificent and seemed like course after course after course. Then, when you were stuffed to the gills, an enormous bowl of fresh fruit was brought to the table. We would just look at it and wonder why, because nobody was hungry. I recall the décor and atmosphere were just incredible. It was dark. They had white tablecloths and, as I remember, we sat in the little coves at round tables. I also remember there were guys going around playing instruments—Italian music—and the whole place just drew you in. The waiters were extremely warm and friendly and just couldn't do enough for you. My brother and sister and I were fascinated by the place and when we would go, we wondered if we might see gangsters there. You know, the lighting, the constant pouring of the wine, the food, the coves, the whole thing—you felt like you were getting just a little taste of what it would be like to be in Italy."

Dan O'Day: "Rosebud on Taylor Street is a very popular place with great food and perfect for people watching. A co-worker friend of mine and I went there one Friday night. He was driving, pulled up in front of the restaurant, opened the door on his side of the car, and just hopped out. 'What are you doing,' I asked. He said they had valet parking attendants who knew whose car was whose and not to worry. We went in and it was jammed. The bar was four-deep. This is a celebrity-type place and when we got in, who was sitting all the way in the back of the restaurant? Tony Bennett! He used to frequent the place when he was in Chicago. The place was abuzz and you could really feel the charge of high energy. All of the help there were really friendly. In fact, the waitress began telling me about her divorce problems. Just a really different kind of place, where I had one of the best steaks of my life…and imagine, in an Italian restaurant, no less!"

Phil Smidt & Son began with a modest eatery in 1910. Though located in northwest Indiana, its lake perch, frog legs, and gooseberry pie were enjoyed by generations of Chicagoans returning home from Michigan resorts. When the nearby Chicago Skyway and Indiana Toll Road improved access to the area in the mid-'50s, the restaurant was expanded to accommodate the crowds. Business dwindled after a floating casino opened next door, and Phil Smidt's closed in 2007 (Eric Bronsky photos).

Betty Schaffel: "I remember going to Armando's, an upscale Italian restaurant on Rush Street. The waiter brought a bottle of wine to the table. He poured a small amount into my husband's glass and stood there. My husband was looking at him as if to say, 'Why don't you pour some for the lady, too?' I said, 'I think you are supposed to taste it,' and he did, and it was fine."

Bob Rubin, Elk Grove Village, IL: "A favorite of ours was Armando's on Rush and Superior—Italian type food. They had a 26 Table when you walked in— it was a dice game. My brother and I knew the owners very well, and quite often we could walk in when there was a long line, and one of the owners, Pete, would see us and say, 'Oh, Mr. Rubin, your table is ready.' Sometimes there would be as many as eight of us and we hadn't called ahead, but apparently we had some clout. Of course, he knew that we would spend a lot of money on food and drinks, and the food was always excellent. A specialty was their shrimp cocktail with their own white sauce, and they would make garlic toast that was prepared at your table. It was truly special what they did."

Mike Zissman, Northbrook, IL: "One of my dad's favorite places was Phil Smidt's in Hammond. Back then, if you had family that would go to Union Pier or Michigan City during the summer, that was the migration and you'd always find a reason to stop at Phil Smidt's. The specialties were chicken, perch, and frog legs. They always had a little tray of forshpeis (appetizers)— cottage cheese, beets, and corn with red and green peppers. There was one room that was called The Rose Room because the wallpaper was black except for gigantic pink roses on it. The food was great. You paid one price and it was all you can eat. It was wonderful for getting dressed up and having family get-togethers. We would have a big table with 10 or 12 of us eating together. Great memories."

Bob Bizar, Chicago, IL: "My aunt once took the whole family to Phil Smidt's. Now, I don't eat fish, but everyone else did and the plates kept coming to the table, plate after plate. So, the waitress asked me, 'Do you want perch?' which is what they were known for. I couldn't even look at it, let alone eat it. I asked what else was on the menu and she told me fried chicken. My aunt kept saying, 'Just try the perch, how bad can it be?' I said, 'I don't know. It could be the best thing in the world, but I don't find it appetizing and I'm not eating it.' My wife whispered to me, 'Your aunt is picking up dinner. Taste it.' 'I'm not going near it. I'm going to eat fried chicken and that's it.' So, I went to Phil Smidt's, where people from all over the country would come to have fish and I ordered fried chicken! I was also able to match the pile of plates from the fish—it was that good."

Cheap and Casual Classics

There were Jewish delicatessens, including Ashkenaz, Bob Elfman's, and Braverman's. Manny's Coffee Shop & Deli (1942-present) is a melting pot that attracts a diverse cross-section of Chicago's population, exuding the "feel" of a unique Chicago institution (Eric Bronsky photo).

Barbara Doctor: "I had just picked up my in-laws at O'Hare and they wanted nothing more than to go directly to Ashkenaz for a bowl of matzo ball soup. After the waitress brought it, they called her back and complained the soup was cold. The waitress said that it couldn't have been because she just taken it out of the pot. She then proceeded to stick her finger into the middle of the bowl. My mother-in-law was shocked and said that it wasn't appropriate for her to do that. The waitress said, "Well, how would I be able to know if the soup was warm or not?""

Joe Mantegna: "When I was a kid, we would go downtown to the State-Lake Movie Theater. Across the street was Bob Elfman's, a wonderful kosher-style delicatessen. I always ordered a corned beef and egg sandwich. Elfman's is my earliest memory of a deli, and I always looked forward to it. The aroma of kosher-style corned beef is indelibly etched in my mind."

The "Catholic Dog"

In doing the research for this book and interviewing people from diverse sectors of the Chicago area about their remembrances of classic Chicago restaurants, including those in their "growing-up" neighborhoods, an interesting story surfaced. First, a foundational fact: The entire Chicago vicinity consists of a large Catholic population. Up until November 1966, it was considered a sin to eat meat on Fridays, but then, U.S. Bishops, who declared meatless Fridays no longer mandatory, with the exception of the period of Lent, lifted the ban.

So, that's the set-up for what follows. Several of the people we interviewed spoke of living in areas with heavy Catholic populations. During their high school years, they naturally gravitated to local hot dog emporiums where the classic Chicago-style hot dog was the drawing card. These included Hasty-Tasty, Gene and Jude's, and Boza's, among a myriad of others. According to them, when they went to those places on Fridays, their friends who followed the rules of the Catholic religion would order a Catholic Dog. What is this?

As we found out, a Catholic Dog is the bun, the mustard, the relish, the onions, the peppers, the tomatoes, the pickles and of course, the celery salt...but no hot dog! Salvation.

As told by Dick Kuhlman, Bob Kryzak, and Phil Paschke

The Early Classics

BEFORE 1920

A Henrici's menu cover depicted Randolph Street as it appeared in 1868, prior to the Chicago Fire. Along with the requisite steaks, chops, chicken, and seafood entrees, early menus included some then-popular specialties virtually unheard of on today's menus: English mutton chops, steamed finnan haddie (smoked haddock, a Scottish delicacy), broiled shad roe (fish eggs), broiled mackerel, creamed chipped beef, lamb pot pie, pickled lamb's tongue, and fried parsnips. Henrici's had a well-stocked bar, but diners could also choose to wash their meals down with a glass of sauerkraut juice, Horlick's Malted Milk, or egg lemonade (Eric Bronsky Collection).

Chicago has always been characterized by muscular attributes: a gritty industrial façade, rough-and-tumble politics, a spirited citizenry, and an innate ability to rebuild itself, innovate, and flourish. Owing to a strategic location at the hub of the nation's early transportation network, the city rapidly developed as the center of the country's meat packing industry, a position it boasted for nearly a century. Although the industry migrated westward during the mid-20th century, Chicagoans continue to savor juicy steaks and chops at some of the finest steakhouses in the country.

But the city's present-day culinary prowess is not entirely rooted on a foundation of sinew and starch. By the mid-1800s, Chicago's population was becoming increasingly cosmopolitan. As the Union Stock Yards grew and prospered, tens of thousands of foreign immigrants seeking a better life in the new frontier sought jobs in Chicago. The Old World families brought to us the culture and traditions of their homelands including, of course, the food. German, Polish, Greek, Italian, Irish, and Chinese cooking could be found in Chicago's multifaceted neighborhoods 150 years ago, but on account of provincialism and prejudice, it was several decades before ethnic foods would start to bridge cultural boundaries.

The city's initial crop of successful entrepreneurs and leaders settled into fashionable new residential enclaves. Demanding foodstuffs on par with New York, Boston, and other older, well-established cities, Chicago's elite stimulated local market demand for better-quality edibles. The advent of refrigerated railroad freight cars in 1869 introduced a variety of fresh provisions from other parts of the country, stocking not just the privatelarders but also the burgeoning hospitality industry—inns, cafés, and hotel dining rooms. The Palmer House, newly raised from the ashes of the Chicago Fire, introduced an elegant dining room with an extensive menu featuring fresh game. Nearby, the North American Oyster House was serving up a bounty of lobsters, oysters, and fresh fish. A pungent dish of shrimp sautéed in garlic butter and topped with bread crumbs was concocted by a chef at the DeJonghe Hotel and Restaurant.

It's difficult to imagine a time when dining out was not among America's favorite pastimes. Before the 1920s, though, class distinction still prevailed and any semblance of fine dining was considered the realm of the "carriage trade" and well-heeled business travelers. The working class dined out only when necessary, leaning closer to hurried sustenance than gratification, and tending to patronize street vendors and lunchrooms near their places of work. Those mundane establishments, dishing out inexpensive meat-and-potatoes fare to factory and clerical workers, were the predecessors to a genre of large lunchroom chains.

Chicago's earliest restaurants were operated by inns and hotels. During the 19th century, farmers delivering livestock to the Union Stock Yards would stay overnight at the Transit House and enjoy a steak dinner in its dining room (postcard image from Wikimedia Commons).

The Stock Yard Inn that became familiar to generations of Chicagoans replaced the Transit House in 1912. Located at Halsted and 42nd, just south of the International Amphitheatre, the Tudor-style Inn provided lodging and several dining rooms for visiting tradesmen and dignitaries. In later years, its Sirloin Room became one of Chicago's quintessential steakhouses; diners could select their cut of beef from a "throne" of ice and have it branded. The Inn, along with the Stock Yards, closed in 1971 (courtesy of the Chicago History Museum, ICHi-23638).

Janet Davies, ABC 7 Chicago, Host and Executive Producer, *190 North*: "My earliest memory of a Chicago restaurant was when we were living in Osceola, Indiana, located outside Mishawaka and South Bend. My father took us on a trip to Chicago in the late 1950s when I was just five years old. I will never forget that adventure because we ate dinner at the Stock Yard Inn. That was my first memory of a restaurant (I think that the Stock Yards were still open at that time) and can remember this very dark, crowded, and smoky dining room where they served diners huge slabs of delicious beef. I also recall how the wait staff made me feel like a little princess. They provided all the children with a crown, which I think that I still have, and I put the crown on while I was having my big slab of roast beef. I will never forget that because it was quite an experience, and it was the first time I ever had a 'Shirley Temple' cocktail. I can also recall the big gas light lamps outside the restaurant, while inside there was a lot of timber used to create a Tudor-style setting."

Chicago's 19th century elite preferred white tablecloth places but the hoi polloi lunched at storefronts such as these. The M. Jungblut Coffee Shop (right) at the corner of Randolph and Market (now Wacker Drive), and the Quick Service Eat Shop (above) at 218 N. Clark typified no-frills eateries that dished out basic meat-and-potatoes fare to the working class during the post-Fire years. Places like these were the ancestors of lunchroom and fast food chains (Eric Bronsky Collection).

Gender segregation was commonplace. Boisterous lunchrooms, saloons, taverns, and pubs which catered to men typically subjected women to disdain or showed them to the door. Some of the larger early restaurants, like H. M. Kinsley's or Rector's Oyster House, offered separate dining rooms for ladies or gentlemen in addition to their main dining rooms. Women eventually opened their own cafés, and later on, State Street's department stores accommodated shoppers with grand tea rooms. The exclusion of women from Chicago's last strictly male bastion, the Berghoff Men's Bar, was finally toppled by the feminist movement in 1969.

As Chicago evolved into a major hub for transcontinental rail travel, travelers passing through Chicago seldom had time for a relaxed sit-down meal. Some years before Fred Harvey introduced what was to become the first national restaurant chain, savvy entrepreneurs were selling "lunches put up in boxes or baskets" from a counter or window. These venues were surely among Chicago's first take-out or self-service eateries, a concept which evolved into cafeterias, buffets, luncheonettes, and much later, fast food restaurants.

The World's Columbian Exposition of 1893 fueled both local and national interest in gastronomy. In some ways resembling today's Epcot Center, this sprawling fair, with its cornucopia of ethnic villages and diverse cuisines, helped to break down provincial barriers and introduce heretofore unfamiliar fare and preparations to Chicago. Following the Exposition, the Loop began to blossom with German, Chinese, Italian, and other ethnic eateries. Their large and remarkably opulent dining rooms featured "Americanized" menus which offered more variety than traditional meat-and-potatoes fare. There was also live entertainment in the form of orchestras and dancing.

Chicago's perceived reputation as a hardscrabble frontier town eroded as the central part of the city became increasingly sophisticated and more accessible to outlying neighborhoods by means of public transportation. The menus of the finer restaurants at the turn of the century displayed a breadth of variety, sophistication, and creativity that seems amazing by current-day standards. Multicourse menus were the rule, cleanliness and safe food handling were crucial, and dining rooms had to be attractive and comfortable—by then, restaurateurs knew that the visual aspect of fine dining was as essential as serving tasty, well-prepared food. Hand-colored postcards reveal palatial dining rooms appointed with marble or tile floors, custom woodwork, heavy draperies, crystal chandeliers, and luxurious linens.

Restaurants were typically family-owned; corporate ownership and restaurant chains would become more common after 1920. In Western Europe,

Chicago's original Chinatown neighborhood was located along a stretch of South Clark Street near Van Buren. The Shanghai Restaurant remained behind at 506 S. Clark long after other businesses had migrated to the new Chinatown at 22nd Street (Eric Bronsky Collection).

some family-owned restaurants had thrived for hundreds of years, handed down from one generation to the next. In contrast, Chicago has always been characterized by rapid growth and evolving neighborhoods, and the city's restaurant industry has been transient.

So, even the most classic of Chicago's restaurants would typically span just one or two generations. But there were several notable exceptions. College Inn, located inside the Sherman Hotel, lasted nearly 130 years. Henrici's, an immensely popular Viennese restaurant in the heart of Chicago's theatre district, opened in 1868 and thrived until 1962. The original Red Star Inn opened in 1899 in a neighborhood populated by German immigrants, and remained essentially unchanged until the building was condemned for urban renewal in 1970. Madame Galli opened an Italian restaurant in the early 1890s which became a popular celebrity hangout; her grandchildren were still dishing up spaghetti next door to the Cinema Theatre on Chicago Avenue as late as the 1960s.

Just two 19th century Chicago classics remain in operation. In the Bridgeport neighborhood, the tavern known as Schaller's Pump has been operating since 1881. And, at the 1893 World's Fair, four brothers from Germany introduced their brewing craft to Chicago. Their beer proved so popular that in 1898 one of the brothers opened a café at the corner of State and Adams to showcase the family's product. Today, owned and operated by the fourth generation of the founding family, The Berghoff Restaurant continues to serve its namesake beer just down the block from its original 1898 location.

The Sherman Hotel and its restaurants had a storied history. Opened in 1837 at the northwest corner of Randolph and Clark as the City Hotel, owner Francis C. Sherman, a Chicago mayor, renamed it Sherman House in 1844 and established an eatery called College Inn. The original hotel was replaced in 1861, but the second hotel was destroyed by the Great Chicago Fire in 1871.

The third Sherman House was completed in 1873. The venerable College Inn became even more popular after the turn of the century, when live entertainment was introduced (courtesy of the Chicago History Museum, ICHi-64653).

An early postcard image of the College Inn depicted an elegant and sophisticated room (Eric Bronsky Collection).

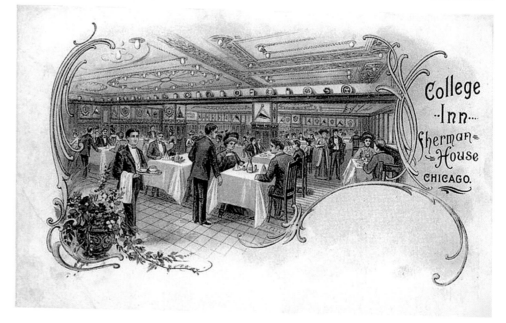

Hotel Sherman
CITY HALL SQUARE
CHICAGO

¶ Faultless service, moderate prices and sincere and unvarying courtesy have made Hotel Sherman the most popular hotel in the West.

¶ Seven hundred and fifty rooms, each with private bath and circulating, distilled ice water.

¶ Located on City Hall Square, right in the heart of the business and shopping section, within easy walking distance of every depot and every good theatre.

¶ If you appreciate a hearty welcome, perfect service and cheerful surroundings, stop at Hotel Sherman the next time you come to Chicago.

Single rooms with bath— $2.00, 2.50, 3.00, 4.00 and 5.00 a day.
Double rooms with bath— $3.50, 4.00, 5.00 and 6.00 a day.
Suites—$5.00 to $15.00.

Home of the World's Most Famous Restaurant

College Inn

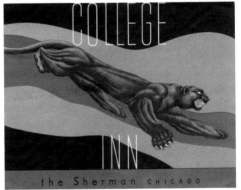

COLLEGE INN
the Sherman CHICAGO

The hotel was rebuilt for the fourth time in 1911. Chicago's present-day City-County Building, located directly across Randolph, was completed earlier that same year. This ad, printed in 1912, gave prominent billing to the College Inn (Eric Bronsky Collection).

A stylish College Inn menu from the 1950s featured Chef Joe Colton's legendary chicken à la King, prepared with his own chicken broth. Complete dinners consisting of an appetizer, entrée, vegetable or potato, dessert, and beverage cost $2.95. Although the Sherman House is long gone, College Inn Chicken Broth is still available through grocery stores (Eric Bronsky Collection).

In 1925, the existing structure was greatly expanded to become the largest hotel west of New York City. The College Inn's impresario was Ernest Byfield, an innovative genius who introduced, among other things, an indoor ice-skating rink. As jazz grew in popularity during the 1920s, he brought in popular band leaders like Isham Jones, giving many Chicagoans their first exposure to this lively style of music. In later years, this room featured musical revues and dancing. Other memorable restaurants and lounges at the Sherman House included Well of the Sea, Celtic Café, the Dome, and the Scuttlebutt. The Sherman, shown as it appeared in 1973 shortly before closing, is now the site of the James R. Thompson Center (Paul Facuna photo, courtesy of the Chicago History Museum, ICHi-18383).

Potter Palmer's first hotel was also lost to the Chicago Fire. It was rebuilt, opening in 1875. This artist's rendering depicts the hotel's dining room circa 1876. The glorious setting, together with fine cuisine served course-by-course, helped dispel Chicago's image as a rough-and-tumble frontier town. This room was the site of a banquet attended by Ulysses Grant and Mark Twain, among other celebrities, in 1879 (courtesy of the Chicago History Museum, ICHi-31461).

The North American Oyster House, at the northwest corner of State and Monroe, received daily shipments of fresh fish, seafood, and game. It was billed as "The only high-class café in the world serving a whole lobster for 50¢." Its cavernous main dining room, shown in this 1910 postcard view, seated 1,000 and was adorned with bird's eye maple, mirrors, white tablecloths, and a mosaic tile floor (Eric Bronsky Collection).

Dating to 1892 and improbably tucked away at the end of a short cobblestone alley known as Pickwick Lane, Colonel Abson's English Chop House was surely one of Chicago's more unusual restaurants. A spiral stairway connected the ground-level bar with the up-stairs dining room and kitchen (courtesy of the Chicago History Museum, ICHi-65654).

The diminutive brick building housed a Prohibition-era speakeasy and other restaurants in later years. Remarkably, this 19th century real estate anomaly has been preserved. Now known as 22 E. Jackson and considered the smallest building in the Loop, it is presently vacant (Eric Bronsky photo).

Philip Henrici was only 23 when he
opened his first eatery in Chicago
in 1868. His Viennese restaurant with
its rich pastries would soon ascend
to become one of Chicago's most popular
restaurants of all time. By 1893, it
occupied a storefront at 71 W. Randolph
in the heart of Chicago's developing
theatre district. The classic old-world eatery
thrived here until 1962, when the entire
city block was razed to make way for
construction of today's Daley Center
(Eric Bronsky Collection).

Henrici's main dining room was patterned after the spacious, elegant dining halls of 19th century Austria replete with large original oil paintings. The restaurant's motto, "No orchestral din," ensured that diners would be able to focus on fine food and quiet conversation without the distraction of loud music (Eric Bronsky Collection).

To commemorate Henrici's 75th Anniversary in 1943, the restaurant published a souvenir booklet containing stories and anecdotes about some of the restaurant's fabled employees and customers (Eric Bronsky Collection).

HENRICI'S 75TH ANNIVERSARY

Whenever Italian tenor Enrico Caruso performed in Chicago, he would dine at Madame Galli, one of Chicago's first Italian restaurants. According to lore, when the restaurant's owner lamented, "I would give the whole world if I could sing like you," the great operatic star chortled, "Madame, I would give the whole world if I could cook spaghetti like you!" Opened in 1893 and originally located at 18 E. Illinois Street, Madame Galli later relocated to larger quarters next door to the Cinema Theatre on Chicago Avenue, just east of Michigan Avenue (George Krambles photo, Peterson-Krambles Archive).

Chicago's population of German immigrants swelled during the late 19th century. The Germans were adept as chefs and restaurateurs, and some of their eateries soldiered on long after the surrounding neighborhoods changed. A prime example was The Golden Ox, which stood in the shadow of the Cabrini-Green Housing project for decades. But, not to be forgotten was the legendary Red Star Inn. It opened in 1899 at 1528 N. Clark in what was a primarily German neighborhood, but the street gradually transgressed into a slum. Urban renewal that began in the early 1960s resulted in the systematic demolition of the surrounding buildings. Despite the protest of preservationists, the Red Star Inn was ultimately doomed. The building to the right in this photo—the Germania Club—won landmark status. This last remaining vestige of the old German neighborhood is now surrounded by Carl Sandburg Village (Hedrich-Blessing photo courtesy of the Chicago History Museum, HB-23892-F).

The Red Star Inn closed on Wednesday, February 11, 1970. The menu on that final day featured the restaurant's usual broad selection of entrees and side dishes (Eric Bronsky Collection).

"The Red Star Inn"

1528 N. Clark St.
Chicago, Ill.

CARL GALLAUER
Founder

ESTABLISHED
1899

Phone
WHitehall 4-9637

MINIMUM CHARGE
$1.00 PER PERSON

Appetizers
Shrimp Cocktail 1.20
Anchovy Canape 1.25
Marinated Herring 1.20
Stuffed Celery 1.10
Orange Juice .... .45
Imported Sardines with Toast .. 1.30
Stuffed Olives .... .60
Dill Pickle, Kosher .... .60
Tomato Juice .... .45
Celery or Green Olives .... .60
Ripe Olives .... .60
Green Onions .... .40
Radishes .... .40

Vegetables
Corn Saute, Peppers, Casserole .80
Stewed Tomatoes .... .70
New Peas .... .70
Red Cabbage .... .60
String Beans .... .60
Sauerkraut .... .55
Spinach .... .70
Cauliflower or Lima Beans .... .70
Smothered Onions .... .60
French Fried Onions 1.20

Potatoes
Hashed Browned .... .75
American Fried............. .65
Whipped or Boiled .... .40
Potato Dumpling .... .70
French Fried .... .60
Au Gratin................. .65
Cottage Fried .... .90

Salads
Red Salmon Salad 1.75
Tuna Salad 1.75
Shrimp Salad 2.25
Hard Boiled Egg Salad 1.40
Pickled Beets .... .40
Head Lettuce .... .55
Combination .... .75
Thousand Island Dressing .35
Sliced Tomato................. .60
Cheese or Bacon Dressing ...... .40

Sandwiches
IMPORTED BONELESS
SARDINES (Box),
COLE SLAW 1.65
BROILED HAM............... 2.25
TOASTED CHEESE............. 1.00
CORNED BEEF SANDWICH .. 1.95
BACON, LETTUCE AND
TOMATO, MAYONNAISE 1.75
AMERICAN CHEESE.......... .85
COLD HAM............. 1.75
SARDINE (MAINE) .... .85

Desserts
Melon in Season ....
Strawberry Pie .... .50
Cherry Pie .... .50
Apple Pie .... .50
Blueberry Pie................. .50
Stewed Prunes .... .50
Pears .... .50
Peaches .... .50
Royal Ann Cherries........... .50
Special Cheese Cake .... .45
Grapefruit .... .40

Cheese and Crackers
Liederkranz .... .75
American .... .75
Cream .... .65; Camembert .75
Limburger Cheese.............. .85

Beverage
Sweet Milk .... .25
Iced Tea .... .25
Stewart's Coffee with Cream .. .20
Pot of Orange Pekoe Tea ...... .25
Sanka .... .25

Red Star Inn

SOUPS (in Cup)
Ox Tail Soup with Barley		.50
Consomme with Liver Dumpling		.80
Onion Soup ..... .50	Consomme Plain	.50
Lentil Soup with Sliced Frankfurter .50	Noodle Soup	.50
Vegetable Soup Paysanne ..... .50	Clam Chowder	.50

Rolls and Butter, White or Rye Bread 10c. per person
(Plate) 20c. additional)

FISH (Received Fresh Daily)
Broiled Swordfish Steak, Anchovy Butter, French Fried Potatoes, Cucumber Salad 4.00
Broiled Large Lobster Tail, Melted Butter, French Fried Potatoes, Cole Slaw ... 8.25
Imported Brook Trout Fried, French Fried Potatoes, Cucumber Salad 4.10
Imported English Sole (Large Size), Fried in Butter, French Fries, Cole Slaw .. 6.50
Baked Jumbo Shrimps, Chef's Special Cole Slaw, French Fried Potatoes 4.75
Fried Scallops, Tartar Sauce, Potato Chips, Cole Slaw 3.95
Fried Filet of Sole, Tartar Sauce, Potato Chips, Cole Slaw 2.95
Broiled Lake Superior Whitefish, French Fried Potatoes, Pickled Beets 5.75
Fresh Caught Large Wall-eyed Pike, Fried in Butter, Boiled Potato, Cole Slaw . 5.10

EGGS AND PANCAKES
Ham and Eggs, Country Style, American Fried Potatoes	3.30
Omelette with Fresh Mushrooms, French Fried Potatoes	3.25
Bacon and Eggs, American Fried Potatoes	3.00
Scrambled Eggs with Chicken Livers, French Fried Potatoes	3.00
Apple Pancake 3.25	Plain Pancake 2.80
Peach Pancake 3.50	Strawberry Pancake 3.50
Mushrooms on Toast	3.25

COLD DISHES
Cold: Prime Rib of Beef with Remoulade Sauce, Potato Salad and Beets 5.75
Roast Duckling with Apple Sauce, Potato Salad, Cole Slaw 4.25
Boiled Ham with Potato Salad and Cole Slaw 3.15
Brisket of Corned Beef with Potato Salad and Cole Slaw 3.15
Jellied Pork Shanks (2) with Cole Slaw and Potato Salad 3.30
Smoked Beef Tongue, Pickled Beets and Potato Salad 3.15

ENTREES
Sauerbraten (Marinated Pot Roast), Red Cabbage, Potato Dumpling 4.00
Leberkloese with Speck Sauce, Sauerkraut, Puree of Peas, Boiled Potato 3.25
Hungarian Beef Goulash in Casserole with Sauerkraut, Potato Dumpling 4.25
Koenigsberger Klops with Caper, Stewed Lentils and Cauliflower 3.10
Wiener Roastbraten (Potted Steak with Mushrooms), French Fried Potatoes,
    Noodles and Peas 5.25
Braised Sweetbreads in Casserole, Potatoes au Gratin, Cauliflower 3.95
Paprika Veal Chop, Potato Dumpling, Buttered Noodles and Peas 4.25
Grilled Fresh Pig's Feet Deviled, Sauerkraut and Boiled Potato 2.75
Fresh Pork Shanks (2) in Casserole, Sauerkraut, Boiled Potato 3.30
Baked Special Knackwurst (2) with Sauerkraut, American Fried Potatoes 2.95
Kidney Stew German Style in Casserole, Potato Dumpling, Buttered Noodles .. 3.25
Potted Ox Joints in Casserole, Bourgeoise, Mixed Vegetables, Potato Dumpling . 3.60
Spaghetti Caruso with Fresh Mushrooms and Grated Cheese 2.75
Roast Stuffed Wokon Duckling, Apple Sauce, Braised Red Cabbage,
    Candied Sweet Potato ..... à 4.25
Zwiebelfleisch au Gratin, Buttered Noodles and Peas 4.10
Roast Young Pork Loin, Apple Sauce, Candied Sweet Potato, Braised Red Cabbage 3.95
Fresh Spareribs with Sauerkraut and Whipped Potatoes 3.95
Hoppel-Poppel (Scrambled Eggs, Frankfurters, Mushrooms, Onion), American Fries 3.25
Braised Fresh Calf's Tongue with Raisin and Almond Sauce, Buttered Noodles .. 3.20
Roast Prime Rib of Beef au Jus, French Fried Potatoes, Brussels Sprouts 5.75
Fresh Chicken Livers Saute with Apples and Onions, Buttered Noodles 3.60
Schnitzel a la Holstein with American Fried Potatoes and Fresh Peas 4.90
Smoked Thueringer Sausages with Sauerkraut and Whipped Potatoes 2.95
Wiener Schnitzel with American Fried Potatoes, Pickled Beets 4.15
Fried Calf's Liver with Onions, Bacon, American Fried Potatoes 4.50

FROM THE BROILER
Filet Mignon, Mushroom Cap, Onion Rings, Potato au Gratin, Brussels Sprouts . . 8.25
Steak Sandwich with Grilled Onions, French Fried Potatoes, Cole Slaw . . 6.25
Prime Sirloin Steak, Mushroom Cap, Smothered Onions, French Fried Potatoes . 7.50
Double Lamb Chops, Mint Jelly, Braised Green Beans, Potatoes au Gratin . 5.65
Double Sirloin Steak for Two 15.00
Broiled Pork Tenderloin with Apple Sauce, Fried Sweet Potatoes, Red Cabbage . 4.25
Pork Chops (2), Apple Sauce, Fried Sweet Potatoes, Braised Red Cabbage . 4.75
Rump Steak, Smothered Onions, French Fried Potatoes . 5.95
Hamburger Steak, Smothered Onions, American Fried Potatoes, Cucumber Salad . 3.75
Hamburger Steak Sandwich, Grilled Onions, French Fried Potatoes, Cole Slaw . 3.15
Broiled Fresh Thueringer Sausages (2), Sauerkraut, Whipped Potatoes 2.95

No Substitutions

Single Portion Served for (2) 25c. additional

Not Responsible for Loss or Exchange of Personal Property

Open Every Day Including Sundays and Holidays

BAKED FRESH JUMBO SHRIMPS, CHEF'S SPECIAL, FRENCH FRIED POTATOES, COLE SLAW $4.75

Schaller's Pump is currently the oldest continuously operating dining establishment in Chicago. A fixture of the Bridgeport neighborhood since 1881, this tavern was a speakeasy during Prohibition. It remains a favorite of local politicians and White Sox fans for its historic flavor and comfort foods (Eric Bronsky photo).

The Berghoff Restaurant did not become one of Chicago's most enduring and iconic dining destinations by chance. In operation since 1898, it is presently owned and operated by a fourth generation of the Berghoff family. The restaurant weathered turbulent times, maintaining its old-world traditions into the 21st century. It became noteworthy for obtaining liquor license no. 1 after Prohibition ended, and was later known for operating the last men's-only bar in Chicago. But, more significant was the restaurant's reputation for pleasing Chicagoans' palates at down-to-earth prices—long lines often spilled out onto the sidewalk. Only in later years when traditionally heavy German cookery waned in popularity did the restaurant bow to modern trends.

The Original Berghoff Bar with License No. 1

The Premier Bar of America

A Section of the Main Floor Dining Room

What is remarkable about this early 20th century postcard view of the bar and dining room is that the historic decor, with its oak paneling, vintage light fixtures, and murals has remained essentially intact to the present time (Eric Bronsky collection).

Perhaps the jolly Art Deco illustration on the cover of a 1941 menu characterized the archetypical Berghoff customer. In addition to hearty Teutonic fare, the menu also listed a bevy of fresh fish and seafood entrees, plus an extensive beverage list featuring Berghoff beer and private stock whiskey (Eric Bronsky collection).

Marshall Field's Men's Grill, located on the sixth floor of the Annex building housing Field's Men's Store (long since consolidated with the main store), featured an enormous Tiffany dome and fountain (Eric Bronsky Collection).

Among the first and surely Chicago's best-known department store restaurant is the Walnut Room, which opened on the 7th floor of Marshall Field & Co. in 1907. This spectacular dining room with its well-maintained wood paneling, European chandeliers, and regal atrium was decorously called a "tea room" even though it served a full menu. Though its kitchen was not the most innovative in town, a smattering of dishes, including Mrs. Herring's chicken pot pie, became local favorites. What made the Walnut Room special were the many seasonal events it hosted, especially the tradition of dining under the "Great Tree" during the holidays. Macy's acquired the State Street store, including the Walnut Room, in 2006 (Eric Bronsky photo).

As State Street department stores grew in size and amenities, they began operating their own restaurants and bakeries to encourage customers to linger. They offered tea rooms, which catered to women and families, and grill rooms, which catered to businessmen. As time went on, cafeterias and snack bars were added to provide less formal options.

1920—1950

1920—1950

The Roaring Twenties was a momentous decade for Chicago's restaurants. Discretionary spending among the middle and working classes increased, and fine dining was no longer limited to just the wealthy; it was becoming fashionable for families to dine out, especially on weekends. But, competition from inexpensive and informal restaurants, particularly cafeterias and early chains such as Pixley & Ehlers, Thompson's, Triangle, Harding's, and B/G, was intensifying. Today, Margie's Candies, Green Door Tavern, and Valois Cafeteria (all opened in 1921); and Lou Mitchell's (1923) remain popular Chicago classics from that era. Ultimately, passage of the Volstead Act in 1919 prohibiting the sale of intoxicating beverages in restaurants, plus consumer protection laws and pressure from organized labor to improve working conditions and industry standards, squeezed many of the white tablecloth places out of business.

Large-scale migration of retail stores and restaurants from downtown to suburbia would not begin until the 1950s, but by 1920, some Loop area restaurants and retail stores were pinched by escalating rents and narrowing profit margins. Chinese restaurants abandoned South Clark Street for the new Chinatown neighborhood at 22nd and Wentworth; Won Kow is today the oldest restaurant in Chinatown, having opened in 1927. Some of the old mansions along Rush Street, vacated when the wealthy moved on to trendier neighborhoods, were refurbished into elegant restaurants. Several of those

Won Kow is the oldest restaurant in Chicago's Chinatown neighborhood. An extensive menu of well-prepared and reasonably priced dishes, both authentic and Americanized, has attracted a steady following. The building's façade is essentially unchanged since 1927 (Eric Bronsky photo).

mansions continue to house some of the city's finer restaurants today.

Fine dining establishments came up with novel ways to attract business. Tableside preparation, once exclusive to places like the Palmer House, became more common. Some restaurants took their cue from the fanciful décor of the then-new Balaban & Katz movie palaces, whose elaborate interiors evoked a sense of escape to another time or place. Using food, décor, servers' costumes, and live entertainment to create an immersive experience, these places were among the earliest "theme" restaurants. The Ivanhoe Restaurant was one such example. Opening as a speakeasy in 1920, it evolved into a romantic celebration of medieval times complete with a spooky catacombs-themed bar in the basement.

Many eateries became classics by being unique and drawing attention. The Empire Room in the Palmer House (1925) became world-famous by showcasing legendary movie, radio, and television personalities for over 50 years. The J. H. Ireland Oyster House (1906) had several nautical-themed formal and informal dining rooms together with "open" kitchens, a new concept for the time, and a "Lobster Grotto," whose focal point was a live lobster tank. Though gone for many years, Ireland's was a prototype for many of today's most popular seafood restaurants.

Live music, dancing, and cabaret were already in vogue at coffeehouses, taverns, and hotel dining rooms when one especially innovative restaurateur

Stepping into Margie's Candies is tantamount to traveling back in time 90 years—the business is still owned by the Poulos family and the original 1921 décor remains largely intact. Famous for handmade confections and ice cream, this Bucktown legend was visited by personalities as diverse as Al Capone and The Beatles through the years (Eric Bronsky photo).

Built in 1872, this wood-frame building located in what is now the River North neighborhood has been home to The Green Door Tavern since 1921. During Prohibition days, the tavern was an Italian restaurant and speakeasy. Its quaint interior is crammed with historic artifacts (Eric Bronsky photo).

almost single-handedly nurtured the start of the Big Band era. Hosting live performances and radio broadcasts in the shadow of the Wabash Avenue 'L,' Otto Roth and his Blackhawk Restaurant achieved world recognition. Roth was instrumental in launching the careers of several of Big Band's most talented stars.

Paradoxically, some restaurants profited handsomely from the ban on alcohol. Al Capone and rival gangsters built fortunes through selling alcohol in Chicago and elsewhere, giving rise to a network of illicit speakeasies and clubs with ties to organized crime. A few of the restaurants, particularly Colosimo's on South Wabash, became revered classics because they romanticized and fine-tuned Italian food and wine to American palates. Whether this indirectly helped to make Italian restaurants hugely popular in Chicago is open to speculation. The decade saw the arrival of Como Inn (1924), Italian Village (1927), and Bruna's (1933).

The Great Depression was not the nadir of Chicago's restaurant industry as compared to manufacturing and other business sectors which fared worse. Nonetheless, some restaurants closed while others survived by lowering prices and offering other incentives to attract customers. The repeal of Prohibition in 1933 helped to avert a prolonged slump.

In fact, a surprising number of new places not only opened during this era but continued to flourish decades later. Among the favorites were Chez Paree (1932), Riccardo's (1934), Jacques (1935), Kungsholm (1937), the Pump Room (1938), and the city's first South Seas-themed restaurant, Don The Beachcomber (1940). Several current-day classics which got their start during the Depression include Twin Anchors (1932), the Cape Cod Room (1933), Billy Goat Tavern (1934), Miller's Pub (1935), and Hackney's on Harms (1939).

It was during the Prohibition/Depression era that Chicago travel author and gastronome John Drury wrote a definitive book extolling Chicago's restaurants. Published by the John Day Company in 1931, *Dining in Chicago* described many of the city's outstanding restaurants of that time, including casual and suburban eateries, in detail. Drury enlisted a fellow author to write the book's foreword, which opens dynamically:

"On reading over the text of John Drury's book one is not merely persuaded that Chicago is a place to stop for more than a sandwich and a cuppa coffee. From page to page he hammers home the evidence that cooking skill and kitchen science has drifted to Chicago from the continents of Asia, Europe, Africa and the archipelagoes of the seven seas..." —Carl Sandburg

Lou Mitchell's on Jackson Boulevard near Union Station has been serving its breakfast and lunch classics to generations of travelers, commuters, politicians, and celebrities since 1923. Moved across the street to its present location in 1949, the iconic coffee shop is imbued with the lore of Route 66. It is listed on the National Register of Historic Places (Eric Bronsky photo).

And, in his introduction, Drury colorfully boasted:

"If you think that Chicago, from a gourmet's point of view, is nothing more than a maze of red-hot stands, chili parlors, cafeterias, barbecue stalls, one-arm joints, chop suey restaurants, counter lunch rooms and all other such human filling stations, artistically embellished with bullet holes, you're as mistaken as Columbus was when he started out on his trip to India the wrong way. Engage in an earnest trip of exploration about the town and you will find, as with Old Chris, a whole new world—a world of epicurean delights that you never thought existed in the City of Winds. We will admit, of course, that the human filling stations are here and in abundance, too, just as they are in New York, New Orleans, or San Francisco; but Chicago, like these other cities, can also boast of first-class restaurants that would delight the heart and palate of the most fastidious and cosmopolitan of gourmets."

Chicago's Century of Progress Exposition in 1933–34 further buoyed optimism, prompting many restaurants to update their décor and kitchens. The futuristic Streamline Moderne style, popularized by the Exposition and designers such as Otto Kuhler, was embraced by both individually-owned restaurants and large chains. Innovations, including neon signage, recessed lighting, stainless steel kitchens, and air conditioning, once considered luxuries, became ubiquitous.

The demands of World War II nearly tripled restaurant business, but the downside was food and labor shortages. As military operations overseas ramped up, local food shortages became more onerous. This, along with a curb on imports, led Chicago's chefs to devise some creative recipes to work around unavailable staples. Menus of that era featured salads, seafood, pasta, and omelets. Fish and fowl, when in short supply, were extended in the form of richly sauced stew or casserole dishes such as chicken à la King, chicken tetrazzini, or seafood newburg. Some of the popular fish dishes of that era, particularly finnan haddie and shad roe, are practically unheard of in Chicago today.

A 1943 menu from The Blackhawk unapologetically headlined, "MEAT SERVED ONLY WHEN AVAILABLE." A discreet note on Ireland's menu from the same time period implored, "Please cooperate in using only one pat of butter." Henrici's message had a gentler tone:

"This is not an apology for any war-necessitated deviations from our established reputation of lavish menus and conscientious service, but an assurance that we are planning for the day when all your favorite dishes [and] all the services that you've come to look for at Henrici's will be here for your enjoyment again."

In spite of wartime challenges, new restaurants continued to open at a brisk pace during and after the country's involvement in the war, most notably Gene & Georgetti (1941), Binyon's (1941), Manny's (1942), Pizzeria Uno (1943), Shangri-La (1944), and Fritzel's (1947). Food and labor shortages extended past the war's end and inflation began to drive up costs. Commercial sources of prepared foods, including frozen and bakery items, were becoming available, often at prices competitive with fresh or raw ingredients. Restaurants would come to rely increasingly on such convenience items to reduce expenses, but the downside was that fewer menu items tasted— or could be truthfully advertised as—fresh.

Ivanhoe, begun as a speakeasy, evolved into a neighborhood family restaurant patterned after Sir Walter Scott's fantasy novel about medieval England. The contemporary cuisine did not allude to the past, but the restaurant was noted for its unique atmosphere, the adjoining Ivanhoe Theatre (opened in 1966), and for being child-friendly.

3000 North Clark Street
Chicago

As hyped on this 1948 menu: "Strolling from room to room is like passing through the glorious enchantment of long ago. The Catacombs with its weird passages and haunting skeletons, Friar Tuck's Cellerage and the Dungeon Bar, the Black Knight's Inn, and Sherwood Forest are but a few of the attractions of this interesting Supper Club, which makes an evening here adventurously different" (Eric Bronsky Collection).

The restaurant closed in 1975, and a Binny's Beverage Depot presently occupies its space. Happily, Binny's preserved the restaurant's castle façade. The old Catacombs Bar, shown in this early view, is now a tasting room (Eric Bronsky Collection).

The multi-room J. H. Ireland Oyster House, or Ireland's, was patterned after sprawling late-19th century classics Rector's and the North American Oyster House. Even during the Depression, people packed the dining rooms for the $2.75 lobster shore dinner and the planked Lake Superior whitefish. The Lobster Grotto room featured a live lobster tank (Eric Bronsky Collection).

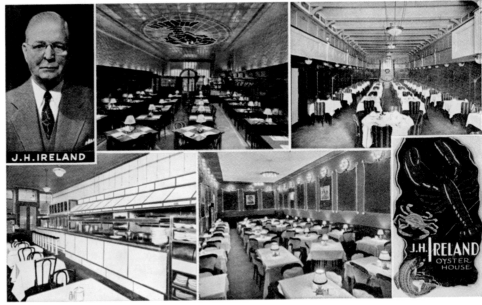

Supper clubs with big-name entertainment boosted several downtown hotels to international fame. The College Inn in the Sherman Hotel, the Terrace Garden in the Morrison Hotel, the Boulevard Room in the Stevens/Conrad Hilton Hotel, and the Empire Room in the (1925) Palmer House shown in this postcard view were among the classics. The latter's splendid French Empire décor was the setting not only for the hotel's sumptuous cuisine but a parade of stars over the years including Liberace, Jack Benny, Tony Bennett, Carol Channing, Jimmy Durante, Jerry Lewis, George Burns, Wayne Newton, Perry Como, Nat King Cole, and Louis Armstrong. Reserved for banquets and weddings since 1978, this room has been fully restored to its early splendor (Eric Bronsky Collection).

Chicago's earliest lunchroom chains could be considered classic because they set a benchmark for plentiful food, fast service, contemporary décor, and modest prices. Several of these eateries were once clustered along a stretch of Clark Street near Madison that was jovially nicknamed "Toothpick Row."

The Pixley & Ehlers and B/G Restaurant chains popularized sandwiches at rock-bottom prices in Chicago long before today's fast-food hamburger chains rose to dominance. The B/G diner, shown here, stood at 30 W. Monroe Street (Eric Bronsky Collection).

A service counter with its "help-yourself system," white-tiled surfaces, and rows of one-arm chairs were the hallmarks of the earliest Thompson's restaurants. This photo shows one of the chain's lunchrooms at 528 N. Clark. The John R. Thompson Co. began in the 1890s with a single location on State Street; by the 1920s, it had expanded into a national chain with 49 restaurants in Chicago alone. In later years, the Thompson chain operated Chicago's Ontra and Holloway House Cafeterias and also acquired Henrici's before being bought out by Green Giant in 1971 (courtesy of the Chicago History Museum, ICHi-17036).

John P. Harding parlayed his famous corned beef and cabbage recipe into a popular local classic. Harding's Colonial Room, located on the second floor at 21 S. Wabash, was a stately setting where one could indulge in this repast, complete with "boiled potatoes, parsley-buttered and as big as a policeman's fist." The Harding's chain at one time operated nine restaurants in the Loop area plus a butcher shop (Eric Bronsky Collection).

Bigg's featured a verbal menu of continental specialties and an extensive list of vintage wines served in the intimate splendor of an 1874 mansion; it is best remembered as a special-occasion kind of place (John McCarthy photo, courtesy of the Chicago History Museum, ICHi-64652).

L'Aiglon was where the nouveau riche would go to be educated about escargot, pâté de foie gras, fromage, and béarnaise sauce by patient waiters who took the time to explain things. The two conjoined mansions housed a labyrinth of dining rooms connected by corridors and stairways (Eric Bronsky Collection).

Opened in 1935, Jacques was then among a very few places in the central city to offer al fresco dining in a garden courtyard. That and its prominent Michigan Avenue location transcended what restaurant critics derided as faux French cooking (Betty Hulett photo, courtesy of the Chicago History Museum, ICHi-24145).

At the opposite end of the spectrum were Chicago's French restaurants. These were popular among the wealthy and famous who could afford loftier prices and were comfortable with Gallic food and traditions. French restaurants have traditionally focused on the well-heeled Streeterville and Gold Coast neighborhoods, but there was also one noteworthy spot in the Loop— Le Bordeaux. Continental restaurants, with a broader variety of Western European dishes, offered somewhat more familiar and affordable fare.

Betty Schaffel, Buffalo Grove, IL: "We went to Biggs once. It was in an old mansion and I remember the way they presented the meal: 'Tonight we're serving such and such,' and then there was this parade of courses making up the meal. It was like going to someone's house for dinner because they had pretty much decided what you were going to eat that night. But everything was excellent."

Le Petit Gourmet was a downstairs restaurant within Michigan Avenue's romantic Italian Court building. Its cozy atmosphere and varied continental cuisine attracted a literary crowd. In warm weather, customers could dine at small tables in the courtyard. The building was demolished in 1968 (courtesy of the Chicago History Museum, ICHi-23123).

A menu cover from Le Petit Gourmet (Eric Bronsky Collection).

Le Petit Gourmet • Chicago

"Big Jim" Colosimo opened his namesake restaurant on South Wabash Avenue not far from the infamous Everleigh Club in 1910. Despite its nefarious origins, Colosimo's earned a reputation for fine Italian-American cooking. Curiosity, seven-course dinners, and live orchestra music continued to attract crowds to this legend long after the demise of its founder. An early ad boasted, "1,500,000 yards of spaghetti always on hand" (Eric Bronsky Collection).

Chicago's old-school Italian restaurants were friendly and charismatic, and featured generous platters of richly-sauced pasta. The diminutive Italian Village, incongruously shoehorned between two massive Loop buildings, operates three distinctively different restaurants on its three floors. The Village, at the top of a steep staircase, is one of Chicago's most enduring and beloved classics. Operated by the third generation of the Capitanini family, its romantically lit 1927 depiction of an Italian village at twilight is timeless and remarkably well preserved (Eric Bronsky photo).

Twin Anchors was one of several Chicago taverns to open following the repeal of Prohibition. Occupying a corner building erected in 1881, it is perennially popular for barbecued ribs and was also a favorite of Frank Sinatra. Ol' Blue Eyes dined here with his friends over a span of several decades (Eric Bronsky photo).

Classic restaurants at the prestigious Drake Hotel have come and gone, but the intimate Cape Cod Room continues to serve a slice of authentic flown-in-fresh New England-style dining, complete with its original 1933 nautical décor, which is widely emulated by seafood restaurants elsewhere. Remarkably, specialties such as Bookbinder Soup, Lobster Thermidor, and Dover Sole Meunière (prepared tableside) have been on the menu since opening day (Eric Bronsky photo/Collection).

Robert and Max Eitel were brothers and restaurant partners in a family of German émigrés who operated, among other businesses, the Bismarck Hotel. Their restaurants included several dining rooms inside Northwestern Station, the Eitel Restaurant in the Field Building, and also Old Heidelberg. The latter began as a restaurant at the 1933-34 Century of Progress Exposition. It was so successful that the Eitel brothers decided to build a permanent version next door to the Oriental Theatre. The Bavarian beer hall motif did not quite fit in with traditional Loop architecture, but the authentic decor and singing waiters were popular with theatergoers.

Phil Paschke, Lewisville, TX: "My ex-father in law, Warren, served in the Navy during World War II and he was the union rep for Wonder Bread in Chicago. One night, we went out for some kind of celebration and wound up at the Eitel Old Heidelberg. We were all drinking and having a good time, and all of a sudden, Warren stood up and yelled, 'Sink the Bismarck!' I thought we were going to get thrown out of the place. I don't know if there were any Germans in there are the time, but when we walked out of there, I said, 'Warren, I'm proud of you.' He was about six foot five and nobody would mess with him. But I can still picture him standing up with that big stein of beer and yelling, 'Sink the Bismarck!' which was a big German battle ship that was sunk in the North Atlantic during World War II."

The cover of a war-era menu, which featured boiled fresh haddock and seafood salad loaf (Eric Bronsky Collection).

Under new ownership in the 1950s, the restaurant was renamed Allgauer's Heidelberg, and later became a Ronny's Steak House. After several years of neglect, the old façade was magnificently restored and currently fronts an Argo Tea café (Eric Bronsky photo).

RICKETTS

"that popular restaurant"

at the Watertower
103 East CHICAGO Avenue

There were two Ricketts lunchrooms on North Clark Street. Encouraged by their success, Ernest Ricketts opted to build a third, more upscale restaurant to attract fairgoers (Eric Bronsky Collection).

The restaurant was sold in 1952 and became Julian's, later Ballantine's, an English tavern specializing in steaks and chops. Charmet's coffee shop, a longtime Michigan Avenue fixture, is visible at far left in this 1976 view (Sigmund J. Osty photo, courtesy of the Chicago History Museum, ICHi-29721).

This architectural sibling of Old Heidelberg was built in 1933 for the World's Fair trade. It stood on Chicago Avenue directly across the street from the Water Tower until 1977. The entire block was later redeveloped.

John Raklios, a Greek immigrant, established a chain of 25 luncheonettes downtown in the 1920s. In 1936, the Raklios restaurant at 64 W. Adams was refurbished in the Streamline Moderne style. With sleek lines, mirrored surfaces, recessed fluorescent lighting, and lack of ornamentation, the décor appears strikingly spacious and modern by current-day standards (courtesy of the Chicago History Museum, ICHi- 64655).

The Chez Paree was a highly popular supper club that opened in Streeterville in 1932. The club had mob connections, and gambling was conducted in a back room called the Key Club. The long list of entertainers who performed here over the years included the Andrews Sisters, Pearl Bailey, Bobby Darin, Sammy Davis Jr., Milton Berle, Joey Bishop, Bob Hope, Edgar Bergen, Eleanor Powell, and Mickey Rooney (Hedrich-Blessing photo, courtesy of the Chicago History Museum, HB-08380).

following pages
George Soto's sleek Miami Beach Deco-style 885 Club was representative of the ambitious nightclubs that were launched in the Rush Street corridor in the years following the repeal of Prohibition, leading to the transformation of Rush Street into one of Chicago's premier dining and entertainment destinations (Eric Bronsky Collection).

Chicago's main entertainment district, of course, was along Randolph Street. Several great restaurants lined the south side of the street between Dearborn and Clark. Henrici's was certainly well known, but Toffenetti (far left) was extraordinary, too—this location was the flagship of its popular eight-restaurant chain (originally called Triangle) that had a presence at two World's Fairs and was later expanded to include a 1,000-seat restaurant in New York's Times Square. Brilliant restaurateur Dario L. Toffenetti had a talent for conjuring up appetizing descriptions of simple foods—ham became *Hot Roast Sugar Cured Ham* and cantaloupe was elevated to *Heart of Gold Cantaloupe-The Best in the Land*. This entire city block fell to the wrecker's ball in 1962 (Eric Bronsky Collection).

Early 20th century Chinese restaurants in the Loop, such as King Joy Lo and Joy Yen Lo, were quite large, impressively decorated, and first-class in all respects. But Harry Eng's spectacular Hoe Sai Gai trumped them all. The ostentatious marquee practically stole the spotlight from neighbor Henrici's. Inside was not only very good Cantonese food but a sensational Art Deco interior created by L Byron Fanselow at a cost of $60,000 in 1937 (Eric Bronsky Collection).

In 1935, the Miller Brothers opened a pub on Adams Street near Wabash. The Gallios brothers purchased it in 1950, keeping the original name because they supposedly didn't have enough cash for a new sign. As time went on, the pub attracted many loyal customers, among them local politicians and celebrities, including Major League Baseball guru Bill Veeck. Miller's moved around the corner to its present Wabash Avenue location in 1989. This view shows the legendary bar at the pub's original Adams Street location in 1966 (Eric Bronsky Collection).

The Kungsholm Restaurant, housed in the stately Leander McCormick mansion, was not beloved for its Swedish smorgasbord so much as the miniature puppet opera that captivated families from 1941 until 1971 (Eric Bronsky Collection).

The historic mansion has been home to Lawry's Prime Rib since 1974. Lawry's is a national chain headquartered on the West Coast, but this spacious restaurant with its opulent and well-preserved interior has become a Chicago classic. This majestic staircase stands just inside the entrance (Eric Bronsky photo).

Fresh from his success at the Sherman Hotel's College Inn, Ernest Byfield opened the Pump Room at the Ambassador East Hotel in 1938. The chandelier-bedecked room with its topnotch swing bands and turbaned feather-plumed waiters serving entrees on flaming swords was an instant hit with Chicago society. Celebrity sightings here were a daily occurrence. Before air travel became common, Chicago was a stopover point for celebrities traveling by train between New York and Los Angeles, so a visit to the Pump Room was de rigueur. Actor Zachary Scott and actress Joan Bennett with her daughter Shelley were seen dining at the Pump Room during an off-Broadway tour of Bell Book and Candle in the early 1950s (courtesy of Lettuce Entertain You Enterprises).

Chicago's penchant for thick, juicy steaks did not wane even as the city's dining scene ascended culinary heights. Gene & Georgetti is the old-timer of local meat emporiums, having observed its 70th anniversary in 2011. Its wood frame building in River North next to the 'L' dates back to shortly after the Chicago Fire, and the menu, décor, worldly servers, and mover-and-shaker clientele all but scream Chicago-style Italian steakhouse (Eric Bronsky photo).

Besides The Berghoff, other revered German restaurants in the Loop once included Schlogl's, located on Wells Street near Madison; the Walnut Room in the Bismarck Hotel (no relation to Marshall Field's Walnut Room); and Binyon's. The latter was tucked away on Plymouth Court, just a stone's throw from the Federal Building. Nattily attired politicians, attorneys, and judges used to flock here for such specialties as turtle soup spiked with sherry, braised ox joints, and apple strudel. The Binyon family sold the restaurant in 1987, and it closed a few years later (Eric Bronsky photo).

Faced with war-time shortages of meat and other staples, chefs were challenged to come up with recipes that used available ingredients but were tasty and satisfying. When native Texan Ike Sewell moved to Chicago, he knew little about the restaurant business until he met Italian-born actor and artist Ric Riccardo. They experimented in the kitchen of Riccardo's restaurant on Rush Street (itself a classic), slathering tomato sauce, globs of cheese, and a sprinkling of whatever meats or vegetables were available onto a thick, doughy crust. The end result was Pizzeria Uno (1943) and its signature deep-dish pizza, which took not only Chicago, but eventually the entire nation, by storm. Ike posed for this photo in 1980 (Eric Bronsky Collection).

Few hotel dining rooms garnered as much attention as the College Inn, Pump Room or Empire Room, but even the less flamboyant downtown hotels had at least one eatery of note. The Congress Hotel did not have quite the panache of the Ambassador East or Palmer House, but its short-lived Glass Hat Lounge was a gem. This 1950s supper club, decorated in the Art Moderne style, became one of the more popular places in the South Loop to impress a date. Its run was brief, though; this portion of the building was soon gutted to accommodate the widening of Congress Street (Eric Bronsky Collection).

The Blackhawk was the quintessential classic Chicago restaurant of the mid-20th Century on several accounts. It opened in 1920 in a prime location across the street from Marshall Field's and near the burgeoning theater district. The introduction of live dance orchestras in 1926 spun the sedate dining room into a major Loop attraction almost overnight. Live radio broadcasts of Big Band and Swing music soon catapulted the Blackhawk to national fame. When the era of live music ended in 1952, restaurateur Don Roth pioneered the food-as-entertainment concept with innovations such as a rolling prime rib cart, the spinning salad bowl spiel, a well-stocked wine cellar, and courtesy vans to nearby theaters. The Wabash Avenue legend packed in legions of local diners and tourists until 1984. Don Roth's Blackhawk in Wheeling carried on the tradition until bowing out gracefully at the end of 2009.

Blackhawk hired professional artists to design its menu covers. This menu, dated December 1, 1943, featured the art of Fridolf Johnson. The cartoon depictions of sailors wooing women were not considered inappropriate in those pre-women's rights years (Eric Bronsky Collection).

The Wabash Avenue restaurant was a fixture under the 'L' for 64 years. Its marquee and long canopy were visible from blocks away (J. Sherwin Murphy photo, courtesy of the Chicago History Museum, ICHi-27870).

Blackhawk's Indian Room, a favorite of families with small children, shared the same address. Its unusual theme extended to yet another Roth innovation—photo opportunities with Native Americans in traditional dress. Here, an Indian Chief joins a group of children in the early 1950s. The restaurant offered a special children's menu and complimentary toys (Eric Bronsky Collection).

1950—1970

Postwar prosperity ushered in socioeconomic changes that ultimately trickled down to the restaurant industry. A housing construction boom in Chicago's suburbs soon gave rise to expressways connecting the central city with mushrooming bedroom communities. With more families enjoying newfound mobility, outlying restaurants and supper clubs became increasingly attractive destinations for urbanites as well as suburbanites.

A long list of suburban classics that were truly special enough to warrant a trip by automobile during the 1950s included Deer Path Inn (Lake Forest), The Indian Trail (Winnetka), Villa Venice (Wheeling), Hackney's on Harms (Glenview), Fanny's (Evanston), Allgauer's Fireside (Lincolnwood), Plentywood Farm (Bensenville), Russell's Barbecue and Nielsen's (Elmwood Park), the Mill Race Inn (Geneva), Old Prague (Cicero), Mangam's Chateau (Lyons), Willow Brook Ballroom (Willow Springs), the Old Spinning Wheel and the Cypress Inn (Hinsdale), White Fence Farm (Bolingbrook), The Homestead (Blue Island), and Phil Smidt & Son (Hammond).

McDonald's and other national quick-service chains were, of course, rocketing to fame by the mid-1950s, but Chicago had much earlier established its own uniquely local casual food classics. These included The Original Rainbow Cone (1926), Prince Castle/Cock Robin (1928), Al's Italian Beef (1938), Gene and Jude's (1946), and Superdawg (1948).

The air travel boom enhanced convention business and tourism in Chicago, and restaurateurs saw a lucrative opportunity to cater to both business and leisure travelers. Visitors characteristically associated Chicago with steaks and chops, so it was customary for the steak houses to promote their wares aggressively. There were some memorable gimmicks. For example, Barney's Market Club owner, Barney Kessel, couldn't remember customers' names, so he greeted everyone with, "Yes sir, Senator," a gag that began long before the 1950s and somehow lasted for more than 70 years. But there were also flashes of brilliance. When Eli Schulman opened Eli's The Place for Steak in 1966, it was not the restaurant's succulent steaks but his signature dessert—cheesecake in assorted flavors—that launched an empire.

Two more genres of restaurants marketed primarily towards tourism came into vogue. The 1949 musical *South Pacific,* later produced as a feature film, and Hawaii becoming the 50th state, helped to fuel a boom in romantic Tiki-themed restaurants. Don The Beachcomber and Shangri-La, which had become popular during the '40s, were joined by Kon-Tiki Ports, Trader Vic's, Shanghai Lil's, and South Pacific. All of these places served unremarkable Cantonese food, but it was their over-the-top tropical décor, exotic drinks, and occasional live entertainment that elevated them to classic status.

84

Though comparable to some of Manhattan's Runyonesque eateries, Fritzel's (1947–1972) was a uniquely Chicago institution that became a mecca for political and business leaders and the news media in the postwar era. This clubby and, at times, boisterous eatery, under a perpetual cigarette smoke haze, was where men in suits would connect over the proverbial three-martini lunch, and where primly coiffed ladies would schmooze from table to table. In this view, a crowd had gathered in front of Fritzel's for the opening ceremony of the new State Street Bridge on May 28, 1949. (Eric Bronsky Collection).

Then, as the skyscraper construction boom got underway, restaurants with a commanding view of Chicago's skyline sprouted. In the past, these had been limited to exclusive private clubs, but Stouffer's Top of the Rock, perched on the 40th floor of the gleaming new Prudential Building, was the first restaurant of its type in Chicago. Facing the Chicago River was the Executive House Hotel with its 71 Club on the 39th floor. Café La Tour opened on top of the Outer Drive East Apartments in 1963. Once again, view and ambience, not so much gastronomic wonders, were the main draw.

As the popularity of tourist spots and budget-priced family restaurants and chains ascended, the more traditional dining venues appeared to reach a plateau. During the 1960s, Chicagoans tended to equate the pinnacle of gustatory excellence with restaurants having a French-sounding name. The cognoscenti would find sanctuary in emporiums like Maxim's de Paris (1963), which topped a list of dignified dining rooms that included Le Bordeaux, Café de Paris, Jacques, L'Epuisette, Biggs, and Chez Paul.

In her book *Chicago: An Extraordinary Guide*, *Sun-Times* columnist Jory Graham raised the ire of local chefs and owners by writing:

"Overrated is the word for a clutch of Near North Side restaurants with French names. All suffer from ownership that attempts a vaguely Continental cuisine on a mass basis. Evidently the owners have found a success formula based on the old meat-and-potatoes theme: Serve it in sophisticated surroundings at reasonable prices, and nobody will mind."

Moreover, Graham advised visitors to lower their expectations:

"Don't look for haute cuisine. The natives won't, as a rule, pay the price it requires, and neither the expense-account crowd nor the 1,300,000 conventioneers who meet in the city annually want it. Neither, it seems, do most of the six-million-yearly tourists."

Harsh words, to be sure, but other food critics seemed to concur with Graham's blunt assessment inasmuch as they did not perceive Chicago to be on a culinary par with cities like New York and Paris.

Out in the neighborhoods, though, sparks of counterculture began to smolder by the early '60s. Coffee houses catering to bohemian artist colonies had existed as early as the 1920s, but a new genre of restaurants began to emerge in the fledgling years of the pop culture movement. At the time Hyde Park resident Hans Morsbach bought the Medici Restaurant in 1962 for a mere $1,750, he had no experience in the restaurant business, just some ideas for tapping into a vast new market. Within a relatively short time, his undistinguished neighborhood coffee house became a tremendously popular hangout for University of Chicago students (one of its regular customers happened to be a young law professor named Barack Obama). Morsbach soon expanded, opening other Medici restaurants in locations where they were certain to attract a youthful crowd. In subsequent years, Medici's casual atmosphere and funky menu were widely emulated by other restaurateurs.

Also in the early 1960s, the quaint old buildings along Wells Street near North Avenue began to attract hippies. These youths were offbeat but savvy entrepreneurs who transformed storefronts into vibrant boutiques, art galleries, head shops, and unique eateries, reinvigorating the Old Town neighborhood with a carnival atmosphere that attracted droves of locals and tourists. Memorable classics here included Chances R, Fireplace Inn, Pickle Barrel, and That Steak Joynt. In nearby Lincoln Park, Geja's Café introduced young couples to romantic dining with fondue, wine, and live flamenco guitar music.

There were other harbingers of future trends. In 1963, a Hungarian immigrant opened a small continental restaurant on Lincoln Avenue that was definitely not run-of-the-mill. Eager diners stood in line, sometimes for hours, to indulge in The Bakery's five-course prix-fixe menu spiked with Louis Szathmary's colorful presence and persona. This institution brought Chicago its first celebrity chef/cookbook author, and also the opportunity to dine while watching the chef at work in the kitchen.

When brothers Bill and Chris Liakouras opened The Parthenon on South Halstead Street in 1968, their menu included two items that no one had ever heard of before—flaming saganaki and gyros. It was not long before those dishes found their way to nearly every Greek restaurant in the United States.

Other occasional sparks of originality brightened the late 1960s. It was the Golden Age of air travel when Blackhawk Restaurant dinner service went airborne on select American Airlines flights to the West Coast. Flight attendants actually recited the saga of the spinning salad bowl and trundled a small version of the prime rib cart down the aisle! This unique service lasted for about a year and a half.

Meanwhile, the decline of the Loop area as a dinner and entertainment destination steepened. This was attributed to several socioeconomic factors, but ironically it was misguided urban renewal that hastened the transformation of fraying streetscapes from energetic to bleak. The new office towers that replaced older buildings offered scant retail space at sidewalk level, and downtown rents were soaring. Some restaurants fled the Loop in favor of up-and-coming neighborhoods, while others simply closed. Sadly, one entire city block that was condemned to make way for construction of the Civic

Center (now known as Daley Center) displaced theatre district classics Henrici's and Hoe Sai Gai. So, in the evenings and on weekends, the Loop was increasingly devoid of pedestrian traffic and retail business.

The Great Chicago Fire of 1871, Prohibition, and the Great Depression all exacted a toll on Chicago restaurants. But it was the tumultuous civil unrest of 1968 that sparked an especially abrupt and prolonged downtrend. With people now fearful about remaining downtown after working hours, Loop dinner business crashed virtually overnight. Some restaurants became lunch-only spots and others closed altogether. Not until some two decades later was there a resurgence of dinner business in the Loop area.

Classic dinner spots in Chicago's neighborhoods were not as adversely affected. In those challenging times, personable restaurateurs who not only delivered a quality experience but also made the effort to befriend good customers were among the more successful in the business. One exemplary individual was Eugene Sage, who opened his first restaurant in the Loop in 1959 and later migrated to the Gold Coast with Eugene's, Mon Petit, Sage's on State, and Sage's East. Gene was known to favor political causes and had a terrific sense of humor.

By the end of the '60s, fast-food chains had replaced cafeterias and luncheonettes, coffee shops had replaced lunchrooms, and Chicago's more traditional restaurants were gamely competing with each other in offering quality, value, and an unprecedented variety of cuisines from nearly every corner of the globe. There had been some brilliant innovations, but as yet, no sweeping industry-wide metamorphosis. Old conventions and formulaic presumptions like *"Italian restaurants are supposed to look Italian with red checked tablecloths and candles stuck in Chianti bottles, and serve red sauce"* were becoming hackneyed or clichéd if not dowdy. The table was set for several bold newcomers to step in and turn the restaurant industry on its ear.

Regardless of direction, most main roads linking Chicago to the suburbs hosted one or more classic taverns, family restaurants, or supper clubs worthy of a long drive from the city.

Just north of downtown Evanston and slightly off the historic Green Bay Trail was Fanny's World-Famous Restaurant. Fanny Bianucci began her namesake restaurant in 1946 as a four-table café. Internationally recognized for its cuisine, the restaurant was greatly expanded, prospering even though Evanston was "dry." Fanny enjoyed mingling with her customers and was often seen in the dining room serving extra helpings of spaghetti or pouring coffee, as in this 1962 photo. Although the restaurant closed in 1987, Fanny's salad dressing and spaghetti sauce are still available in local groceries (Eric Bronsky Collection).

Old Prague's distinctive Old World architecture and a highly visible location on 22nd Street (Cermak Road) in Cicero added to its popularity. Opened in 1944, this restaurant specialized in hearty Bohemian cuisine. Its elaborate décor was rich with woodwork, art, and antiques. The building was destroyed by a fire in 1993 (Eric Bronsky Collection).

Chez Paul (1945-1995) was one of Chicago's more enduring—and endearing—French restaurants. In 1964, owner Bill Contos relocated it to the former Robert Hall McCormick mansion on Rush Street, shown in this 2008 photo. The European-style façade and romantic candlelit interior inspired filmmakers; its interior was replicated on a soundstage for filming scenes in *The Blues Brothers* and *Ferris Bueller's Day Off* (Eric Bronsky photo).

Shangri-La opened in 1944 in a freestanding building, previously the Rhumba Casino, on State Street near Wacker Drive. It was popular for its exotic décor, live music, and potent drinks, and had a reputation for very good Cantonese food. Shuttered in 1968, this space was converted to an X-rated movie theater and the building was demolished in 1981 (Eric Bronsky Collection).

Don The Beachcomber, created by Ernest Raymond Beaumont Gantt (who legally changed his name to Donn Beach), was a chain of Polynesian restaurants begun in Los Angeles in 1934. The Chicago branch opened on Walton Street in 1940. This was Chicago's first Tiki-themed restaurant; its exotic décor and Gantt's original rum-based concoctions were emulated by several Chicago restaurateurs and also by the competing Trader Vic's chain. Although this particular spot closed many years ago, Don The Beachcomber restaurants still exist in California and Hawaii (Eric Bronsky Collection).

Barbara Doctor: "I remember the London House from my very first time there. It was winter and my girlfriend and I were on the phone all day talking about how we should dress. I remember they took our coats when we entered and we looked at the menu and our eyes popped out of our heads. You know, steaks at seven dollars! A double baked potato—two dollars! And I'm thinking, 'You can't ask a young man to pay for that kind of dinner.' So, of course, they let us order first and my girlfriend ordered the French-fried shrimp and I ordered the French-fried chicken and each of the boys ordered prime rib. And we just totally looked at each other because we had no idea of what was the right thing or the wrong thing to do. Going back there years later, I ordered the prime rib, too. You bet!"

Dan O'Day: "When I worked at the *Chicago Sun-Times*, I would occasionally tell my dear wife I had to work overtime and a couple of buddies and I would go to the London House for drinks and listen to great jazz. The music would range from Count Basie to George Shearing. One time, my wife came downtown to have dinner with me and we went there. In addition to music, they also had terrific food. George Shearing was appearing and as we were leaving, he was standing out front with his seeing-eye dog. I stopped and said, 'Excuse me, Mr. Shearing, but I wanted to introduce myself and let you know how much I have enjoyed listening to you over the years. My wife is with me right now and I have to admit that sometimes I've come to hear you when telling her I was working late.' He was very gracious and a perfect gentleman in his English ways and said, 'I am very flattered.' He wrote some big songs like *East of the Sun* and, of course, *Lullaby of Birdland*—the biggest. What a thrill it was for me to meet him under those circumstances."

The first venture of nightclub impresarios George and Oscar Marienthal was London House, located in the London Guarantee Building on the windswept corner of Michigan and Wacker. With a more casual vibe than most Loop hotel clubs, this spot featured a menu of local meat-and-potatoes favorites, together with music by some of the best jazz musicians in the country. The Marienthal brothers later added two Rush Street classics to their portfolio: Mister Kelly's and The Happy Medium. London House livened up this corner of the Loop until the early 1970s (Eric Bronsky Collection).

Fritzel's close proximity to Marshall Field's and the movie palaces assured a steady stream of customers from lunchtime through after-theatre hours for its Jewish specialties, egg dishes, and salads. Meals always began with a basket of Fritzel's delectable onion bread.

Fritzel's main dining room
as it appeared in 1957
(Eric Bronsky Collection).

Fritzel's menu dated Saturday,
December 6, 1958
(Eric Bronsky Collection).

Appetizers

Tomato Juice 40	Papaya Juice 40
Fruit Cocktail......85	Bismarck Herring ..85
Marinated Herring .85	Gefilte Fish 85
Sweet Sour Fish 85	Chopped Liver 85
Crabmeat Cocktail 1.25	Shrimp Cocktail ..1.10
Blue Points or Cherrystone Cocktail on Ice ...1.10	

Soups

Cream of Green Pea Soup, Longchamp, Cup ...35
Clear Chicken Broth, Alphabet, Cup 35
Clear Chicken Broth with Egg Flakes, Cup 35
Hot or Cold Beet Borscht, Cup 50; Tureen 95
Poached Eggs, Benedict 2.10
Oyster Stew with Milk 1.60; with Cream 1.85

Salads

Hollywood Salad Bowl 1.75
Mixed Greens with Julienne of Chicken, Ham and Swiss Cheese, Lorenzo or 1000 Island Dressing
Imperial Salad 1.75
Romaine, Chicory and Limestone Lettuce, Sliced Tomatoes, Avocado Pear and Crisp Bacon, French Dressing
New Orleans 1.90
Chopped Hearts of Lettuce, Watercress, Cucumbers, Radishes, Fresh Shrimp and Crabmeat, 1000 Island Dressing
Chef's Special Salad 1.70
Chopped Mixed Greens, Sliced Hard Boiled Eggs, Anchovies and Tomatoes, Garlic Dressing
Chicken Salad (White Meat Only) 2.85
Hard Boiled Eggs, Sliced Tomato, Mayonnaise
Shrimp Salad 2.85
Crisp Lettuce, Ripe Tomatoes, Hard Boiled Egg, Mayonnaise
Fresh Lobster Salad 3.45
Eggs, Tomatoes, Capers, Mayonnaise
Salmon Salad 1.70
Tomato, Hard Boiled Egg, Crisp Lettuce
Salad Fritzel, Special 1.90
(Limestone Lettuce, Avocado, Boiled Egg, Sliced Tomato, Hearts of Palm)
Calif. Fruit Plate, Cottage Cheese or Sherbet .1.75

Desserts

Melons in Season ...75

Cheese Cake 45; Strawberry Cheese Cake 65
Fresh Pineapple ...95   Peach Melba 75
French Pastry 45   Coffee Cake 45
Apple Pie 45   Compote of Fruit ...60
Frozen Layer Cake 50; with Sauce 65
Pound Cake 45   Sliced Bananas 65
Ice Cream: Chocolate or Vanilla 45; Sundaes ..55
Frozen Eclair 65; Baked Delicious Apple 60
Old Fashioned Chocolate Layer Cake 45
Fresh Strawberries, Blueberries or Raspberries .95

Business Men's Special 1.50

Soup du Jour

Julienne of Chicken Chop Suey in Casserole,
Boiled Rice, Fried Noodles, Oriental

Banana Cream Tart   Stewed Fruit Compote

Coffee, Tea or Milk

Club Luncheons

Fried Filets of Lemon Sole, Tartar Sauce 1.80
Broiled Fresh Alaska Halibut Steak,
Lemon Butter 1.80
Omelette with Grilled Sliced Kosher Salami,
Pancake Style 1.75
Roast Prime Sirloin of Beef au Jus, Natural ..2.30
Smoked Brisket of Beef, Hungarian Shallot ..2.30
Sweet-Sour Meat Balls in Casserole a la Fritzel 1.80
Broiled Beef Tenderloin Patties, Bordelaise ..1.85
Baked Sliced Capon on Brochette a la Vileroy 1.85
Broiled Veal Chop with Mushrooms,
Grilled Tomatoes 2.50
Steamed Jumbo Frankfurters with
Baked Beans 1.75
Broiled Sliced Virginia Ham, Pineapple Glace,
Cumberland Sauce 1.80
Cold: Hawaiian Pineapple Stuffed with
Chicken Salad, Garnished 1.90
Choice of Two
Buttered Spring Vegetables
Kernel Corn Saute
Mashed in Cream Potatoes
Hashed Browned Potatoes
Banana Cream Tart   Stewed Fruit Compote
Choice of Ice Cream
Choice of French Pastry 30c. additional
Coffee   Tea   Milk

Beverages

Postum or Sanka ..30	Iced Coffee 35
Milk 25	Coffee, Pot 35
Iced Tea 30	Pot of Tea 30

NO CHARGE FOR EXTRA COFFEE

COCKTAILS and SHERRIES

CHAMPAGNE, Domestic 1.10; Imported 1.50
Daiquiri 80   Whiskey Sour .80   Manhattan ...80
Rob Roy 90   Martini 80   Bacardi 80
Gonzales Tio Pepe, Bone Dry 80   La Ina Sherry, Very Dry ..80
Glutinos Sherry 80   Old Fashioned 80
Harvey's Bristol Cream Sherry 1.00
Harvey's Bristol Dry Sherry 1.00
J. & B. Pall Mall Sherry 1.00
Canadian and Bonded Whiskies 10c. extra
Imported Gins 15c. extra

Hot Sandwiches

(All Hot Sandwiches served with Mashed or French Fried Potatoes)
Hot Roast (Prime Sirloin) of Beef Sandwich 1.70
Hot Turkey Sandwich, Cranberry Sauce 1.65
Hot Sliced Chicken Sandwich, Creamed
Mushroom Sauce 1.75; White Meat 1.85
Hamburger Sandwich, International Club ...1.70
Western Sandwich, Garnished 1.35
Toasted Cheese with Bacon and Tomato 1.25
Fried Ham and Egg Sandwich, Garnished ...1.40
Special Sirloin or Tenderloin Steak Sandwich,
Cole Slaw or Salad and Potatoes 3.50
Club Sandwich, Garnished 1.50
Toasted Cheese on Rye Toast, Grilled Sliced
Ham, Spiced Peaches, Garnished 1.55
(Prime Rib) Sandwich, Salad and Potato ..3.00

Cold Combination Sandwiches

Shrimp Salad Sandwich, Sliced Tomato,
Cole Slaw, Hard Boiled Egg, Mayonnaise .1.85
Beef Tongue and Tomato 1.35
Imported Sardines, Sliced Onion, Cole Slaw .1.70
Brisket of Corned Beef, Dill Pickle 1.35
Chopped Chicken Livers and Sliced Tomato 1.30
Salmon Salad, Hard Boiled Egg 1.35
Chopped Chicken Livers and
Breast of Turkey, Fritzel 1.80
Sliced Chicken Sandwich, Garnished 1.50
Sandwich 201: Virginia Ham, Breast of Turkey,
Swiss Cheese, Cole Slaw, Russian Dressing 1.60
Fresh Nova Scotia Salmon, Cole Slaw,
Sliced Tomatoes 1.85
Genuine Lake Sturgeon with Bermuda
Onions and Tomatoes 2.25
Hard Boiled Egg, Anchovies, Sliced Tomatoes 1.35
Chicken Salad Sandwich, Garnished 1.50
Ham and American Cheese, Garnished 1.35
Saturday, December 6, 1958

Dan O'Day, Gurnee, IL: "The Wrigley Restaurant and the 'Wrig Bar' were very popular among newspaper and ad agency folks. Years ago, the Wrig Bar was basically a men's bar, famous for its martinis. They were great and only 90 cents at the time. When they had to raise the price to $1.15, they apologized to the customers. The gin and vodka they served was Gordon's—not some cheap off-brand stuff. The Wrigley Restaurant also served very good, reasonably priced food. You could get an excellent lunch for seven or eight bucks. Dinner could be a lot more expensive—maybe 12 dollars (wink)! Mr. Wrigley strived to keep the prices down so people would continue to come in. He was quite a gentleman. An interesting note about the Wrigley Restaurant: If you came in through the National Boulevard Bank lobby, you'd notice a big, round table with chairs for eight people. That table was always reserved for Mr. Wrigley in case he needed it after a business meeting upstairs."

Across the river from London House and Fritzel's, the Wrigley Building Restaurant, opened in 1936, also held a special magnetism for the postwar power lunch crowd. Many of the business types who dined here were in the broadcasting and journalism fields. Well-prepared continental and American standards and a seasoned staff who made a point of learning their customers' preferences kept this airy dining room packed at lunchtime (Hedrich-Blessing photo, courtesy of the Chicago History Museum, HB-24252).

Decades before Arnie Morton launched his successful national steakhouse chain, his family operated Morton's Restaurant, located in the Hyde Park neighborhood on Lake Park Avenue, and also Morton's Surf Club on South Shore Drive. Young Arnie learned the ropes by performing a variety of tasks here (Eric Bronsky Collection).

What put Café Bohemia on the local radar was its atypical menu of seasonal and year-round game. Where else could Chicagoans or travelers arriving at nearby Union Station go to satisfy their cravings for specialties such as braised African hippopotamus, roast native beaver, grilled loin of lion, or perhaps just a simple bear steak? (Janet Schleeter photo, courtesy of the Chicago History Museum, ICHi-19784)

Changes to neighborhood restaurants inevitably occurred as a result of ethnic migration. Here is a case where one classic restaurant followed another at the same location: Little Jack's (1905–1960s) was an East Garfield Park classic that attracted a predominantly Jewish clientele and was known for its cheesecake.

In 1966, the storefront became Edna's. Owner Edna Stewart was known not just for her legendary soul food; her restaurant was also a meeting place for leaders of the Civil Rights movement. It closed in 2010 shortly after the owner passed away, but a longtime employee resurrected the business with the same staff and recipes, and Edna's legacy lives on as Ruby's (Eric Bronsky Collection).

Catering Corporation of America operated several restaurants inside the 1 East Wacker Drive (now Unitrin) Building, completed in 1962: Club on 39; The Crown Room (on the 41st floor); a cafeteria plus conference and banquet facilities on the second floor; and The Little Corporal at plaza level. The latter was a coffee shop with a vaguely French theme and an unexpectedly opulent décor that might have pleased even Louis XIV. This view shows the plaza level entrance on Wacker Drive (Hedrich-Blessing photo, courtesy of Chicago History Museum, HB-28090).

Suspended above one dining area was a gigantic replica of Napoleon's bicorn hat. The Napoleonic decor also extended to the clever menu design (Eric Bronsky Collection).

At the opposite end of the spectrum were Chicago's French restaurants. These were popular among the wealthy and famous who could afford loftier prices and were comfortable with Gallic food and traditions. French restaurants have traditionally focused on the well-heeled Streeterville and Gold Coast neighborhoods, but there was also one noteworthy spot in the Loop—Le Bordeaux. Continental restaurants, with a broader variety of Western European dishes, offered somewhat more familiar and affordable fare.

The eccentricity of Chef Louis Szathmary's
The Bakery—its inconspicuous location,
no printed menus, and mismatched
table settings—was part of its charm.
This postcard view of the chef-owned
restaurant that helped to arouse Chicago
from its meat-and-potatoes slumber
spotlights not the dining room but the large
staff and their savory European dishes
(Eric Bronsky Collection).

Chances R, which opened on North Wells Street in 1961, was one of the first arrivals to the fledgling Old Town commercial strip. Intentionally designed to look ramshackle, it featured half-pound burgers, beer on draught, and baskets of peanuts. Customers were encouraged to toss empty peanut shells onto the hardwood floor, a shtick that has been widely copied elsewhere (Eric Bronsky Collection).

La Strada, an Italian restaurant on North Wells Street during the 1960s, was best known for its attractive courtyard entrance. The focal point for al fresco diners along this faux alley was a fireplace behind a waterfall. Later, this restaurant became The Courtyard Inn, a barbecue rib emporium owned by Dick and Jim Novak of The Fireplace Inn (Eric Bronsky Collection).

The Parthenon Restaurant, which opened in 1968 in a modest Halsted Street storefront, played a key role in placing Chicago's Greektown neighborhood on the map. Famous for introducing flaming saganaki and gyros to the world, the restaurant successively expanded and remodeled through the years. Two other longtime Greektown classics, Greek Islands and Rodity's, are located nearby (Eric Bronsky photo).

The first public rooftop restaurants tended to be formulaic or gimmicky. One example was the Pinnacle, located atop the Holiday Inn on Lake Shore Drive. It featured a dining room mounted on a turntable that revolved slowly, emulating Seattle's Eye of the Needle Restaurant and its (then) so-so food.

Completed in 1955, the Prudential Building was then the tallest skyscraper in Chicago. Stouffer's Top of the Rock offered diners an unparalleled view of the lakefront and skyline from the 40th floor and more stimulating menu choices than the other Stouffer's restaurants. In this postcard graphic, note the chivalrous gentleman lighting his companion's cigarette. Stouffer's once operated several restaurants in downtown Chicago. Today, the Stouffer's brand is owned by Nestlé and is strictly a frozen food business (courtesy of Lawrence Okrent).

When the John Hancock building was completed, Davre's (the fine dining division of ARA Services) opened a restaurant on the 95th floor and called it The 95th. Having spent a generous sum on décor, Davre's objective was to upgrade all aspects of sky-high dining. This 1970 publicity photo was taken to show the stylish new waitress uniforms in Davre's plush 96th floor cocktail lounge. Today's Signature Room offers fine cuisine worthy of the spectacular view (Eric Bronsky Collection).

Recent Classics

1970–PRESENT

One of the most important restaurants—and definitely a Chicago classic—that set the framework for post-1970 Chicago restaurants was owned by the legendary Eli Schulman. His son, Marc, has provided an excellent description of the restaurant, Eli, and how it impacted Chicago dining from 1966 to 2005:

Marc Schulman, President, The Eli's Cheesecake Company: "Eli's The Place for Steak was focused on Eli because he was just the kind of icon that no matter what else you came in for (and he served great food), the experience was Eli. He was like an air traffic controller because he would have the people lined up to come in, the activities, the excitement, and his many friendships. It was a generation that included Gene Sage, Arnie Morton, Jovan, Louis Szathmary from The Bakery, and Don Roth. My dad was also very involved in the community and served on the board of McCormick Place. There was a time when the Eisenberg Boys and Girls Club was raising money and dad gave a fundraiser that included Gale Sayers and Brian Piccolo. When Brian became sick, my dad went to New York with them. Although Arnie Morton gets credit for starting Taste of Chicago, we were founding vendors and were there from the beginning. We were on the Chicago Fine Dining List Association and we are the only member that has been at the Taste all these years.

Dad had many followers along with his lunch bunch, including Bernie Judge, Steve Neal, Ed McCaskey, Howard Bednoe, Ben Bentley, and the great Kupcinet. Irv used to meet there once a week, while George Dunne would be at Eli's for Steaks on Monday nights. I saw a doctor the other night who told me that he knew Mike Madigan and that as a young politician he remembers that George Dunne and Ira Kolitz would eat at Eli's on Monday night. And, on a typical day, my dad would either go to a baseball game for a few hours or maybe out to the Arlington Park Racetrack. So, if Eli could get away he would do it, but I think that the restaurant business became the centerpiece of my life when I was growing up.

My father worked every day and night and my mother was there during the day, and, frequently, at night as well. These included social events and whatever occasion was being celebrated at the restaurants. When it closed in 2005, my mother was there for the last day along with key employees and customers. It is something that could come back someday, in the right circumstances.

He liked the cheesecake business because it only involved sending out the product. I remember watching Eli on a Saturday with the reservation sheet and filling in the seating and the in-betweens. And, the other stuff was

a lot like watching Patton getting ready for battle. He was thinking about who would show up, who could eat quickly, how could he fit a five in a four, or how could he put two tables together. Eli didn't like big parties and he had the busboys there because he emphasized the whole idea of speed.

Today, you go into a restaurant and you see plates that haven't been picked up. Eli had the opportunity and the ability to take a good meal and really make it an unbelievable experience, and I think that you would remember the food and clearly remember Eli and what he did in all those other parts. I think that is what he was able to bring to the restaurant business.

He loved Chicago and he loved people. He opened in 1966 during the Mayor Richard J. Daley era and I remember Eli showing me the mayor when he came in for dinner one night although I understand that the mayor didn't go out for dinner that much. It was a Sunday night and my dad used to take Sunday nights off, but when the mayor was at the restaurant, so was Eli. I don't think that my dad ever took Sunday nights off again. He was just always there. But the one thing to note was that when he did go away, he just closed down the restaurant for that time period. Eli's closed each year on Mother's Day, Father's Day, and for three weeks during Christmas. He just said, 'It's December 10, we're done for the year.' He didn't care because he wanted to go to Florida, and if he wasn't going to be in the restaurant, then it was just closed.

I think that Chicago is a great place to do business, and my dad, who passed away in 1988, was definitely a civic leader in the dining community. The city continues to be a culinary city. Eli was dominant in the era where the restaurateur was the star, although there were a few restaurateur/chefs like Jovan and Louis Szathmary, but Eli was a host and a producer like Gene Sage. He was the humanitarian, citizen, and leader and I think that he was someone who was considered to be a trusted advisor. That is what he brought to it, so Eli's was just him. In a lot of ways, people would be willing to pay double or triple or quadruple because he was priceless. And, unlike a Rich Melman or a Larry Levy who focused on creating and duplicating concepts, when Eli had two restaurants, it was hard for him to deal with because he really wanted to be in one place."

After Eli's had been in business for a few years, it is generally agreed by fanciers of Chicago dining that a new period of restaurant development, along with new restaurateurs, began in the early 1970s with the opening of R.J. Grunts by Richard Melman and Jerry Orzoff. This eating establishment would become the first "theme" restaurant opened by Melman and led to the creation of a dining company called Lettuce Entertain You Enterprises, Inc. (LEYE). By 2011, Richard Melman and his numerous partners and

In 1940, Eli Schulman opened his first restaurant, the Ogden Huddle, on Chicago's West Side.

His second restaurant, Eli's Stage Delicatessen, stood on Oak Street near the Esquire Theatre. Eli (center) posed with comedians Joe E. Lewis (left) and Henny Youngman (right).

This ad appeared in *Nightlife in Chicago*, a tourist publication, in 1968.

Eli's The Place for Steak attracted VIP customers and launched the Eli's Cheesecake empire (photos courtesy of Marc Schulman).

investors had opened over 80 dining establishments, not only in the Chicago metropolitan area, but around the country in places like Las Vegas, Phoenix, Minneapolis, Washington, DC, Atlanta, and Santa Monica, California. The general concept behind the LEYE restaurants was for the diner to have fun, along with an enjoyable dining experience at places that have ranged from such establishments as R.J. Grunts, Fritz That's It!, Jonathon Livingston Seafood, Lawrence of Oregano, and the Great Gritzbe's Flying Food Show to Ambria, Un Gran Café/Mon Ami Gabi, The Pump Room, Everest, Tru, Shaw's Crab House, Joe's Seafood Prime Steak and Stone Crab, Brasserie Jo, Hub 51, Paris Club, and L2o.

Richard Melman, Founder and Chairman, Lettuce Entertain You Enterprises, Inc.: "I was born to Morrie and Bea Melman in 1942, and we lived in Logan Square at 3635½ West Dickens. The funny part is that R.J. Grunts, our first restaurant, is also on Dickens. It was such an omen to me when we found that location that I said to my partner, Jerry Orzoff, 'Hey, I grew up on this street!'

When I was very young, my dad and his brother, Art, owned a drug store. They were involved in a number of businesses, so each had a series of jobs which included working in factories and owning a grocery store. I vividly remember accompanying them to their grocery store on Sundays, walking up and down the aisles to marvel at all the food displays, and then—my favorite part—getting to drink a can of Dean's Chocolate Milk.

In the early 1950s, my dad and uncle Art—even though they had never been in the restaurant business—bought a cafeteria across from the Civic Opera House. The fact is they really bought it because there was a dice game they played at the register called *Twenty-One*. Years later, my father told me that the restaurant did so well that one day they decided to forget about the gambling aspect of the business and pay more attention to the restaurant. And that started them in the restaurant business.

They opened Ricky's on Roosevelt and Crawford, and after that, they opened Ricky's on Division and California, at which point they decided to go their separate ways. My uncle Art took the restaurant on Division and California, and my dad kept the one on the West Side. Then, my dad sold his restaurant and opened a new Ricky's on Belmont and Broadway with his good friend and new partner, Lou Greenberg. A few years later, my dad and Lou opened their most successful restaurant, Mr. Ricky's, on Skokie Boulevard in Skokie.

I began working in restaurants when I was 14 years old. During my teens, I had a series of restaurant jobs, ranging from working at Henry's

Drive-In to selling restaurant supplies. When I was 19, I started working for my dad and Lou at Ricky's on Belmont and Broadway. I was doing a relatively good job until I made a big mistake. It was a Sunday, and I was due to work the 8 a.m. to 5 p.m. shift. Unfortunately I neglected to tell my dad that I had to leave for a couple of hours to play on a softball team that was competing for the championship of Grant Park. Well, it was a very busy day at Ricky's and I told the manager that I needed to leave, but would be back in a couple of hours. We won the championship in a doubleheader, and around 2:30, I returned to the restaurant to celebrate with my teammates. My dad was there and was livid because he thought I had been irresponsible. He then fired me. I was so happy we had won the championship, but also felt very bad that I had messed up.

After high school, I went away to college, but was never much of a student, and flunked out after two years. With this failure under my belt, I realized I needed to take my future more seriously, and began to look at the restaurant business as a career. Within a couple of years, I started liking it, and was devoting a lot of time and thought to making my dad's restaurant more successful. I was creating menus, developing systems, and working very hard as a manager at Mr. Ricky's. I was very focused on the restaurant business, and decided to approach my dad and his partner, Lou, about becoming a partner. I would have been happy if they would have sold me 2½% of the business, because, over a five-year period of time, I had saved $10,000 and I was willing to put my money in to buy a piece of the restaurant. They didn't seem to think much of that idea and said they wanted to think about it. They then sat me down and said, 'We want to see you more settled and married before we bring you into the business.' My reaction was that I didn't even have time to date because I was so focused on learning the business. I was shocked and hurt that they couldn't see what I would bring to the partnership.

After my dad and Lou turned my offer of a partnership down, I went back to work, but something had changed for me. In a couple of weeks I decided to leave. I wanted a future and to be a part of something, so I moved to Miami to try to partner with some people there in a restaurant franchise. When this didn't work out, I returned to Chicago and took a job at Robby's Restaurant on Lincoln near Kimball. Bob Saperstein owned the restaurant with his father, and they were wonderful people. Bob discussed the possibility of partnering with me, but, at the time, he wasn't ready to do it.

When I met Jerry Orzoff, I finally found someone who was willing to take a risk on me. Together we opened R.J. Grunts in Lincoln Park on June 10, 1971. More established restaurateurs at that time considered our place to be a big joke. I remember some people thinking that Grunts was a crazy concept, that there was nothing to it and that it was just a fad. But, a lot of younger people were talking about Grunts, and it got to be extremely popular. I believe that our little place started a completely different way of thinking about restaurants in this country.

That's not to say that R.J. Grunts was an overnight success. In fact, for the first eight weeks, there were hardly any customers, and Jerry and I were definitely concerned that the restaurant wasn't going to make it financially. After about six weeks, I felt like such a failure that I started making plans to start working two jobs—one to pay for my living expenses, and one to re-pay the loans that we had taken out to open Grunts. When the restaurant finally took off, we were both so relieved and happy, but I had also learned a lot from this near failure.

I was energized by the restaurant's success and, moreover, it was exciting to discover that I had finally found what I loved to do in my life! I realized that I am well suited for the restaurant business because I am service-oriented and prefer doing favors for others instead of asking for favors.

There is a story behind every restaurant that we opened. After Grunts, our second restaurant came about because of an idea given to us by Fred Joast, who my parents introduced to Jerry and me. Although he was a European-trained chef, Fred was operating the Pickle Barrel where they encouraged customers to throw peanut shells on the floor, just like Chances R, another popular restaurant in the '60s. He helped us out when we opened Grunts and was interested in working more with us. After about a year and a half, Fred found a location for a new restaurant in Evanston in what had been Abner Mikva's congressional headquarters on Chicago Avenue near Davis. He came to me and said, 'Rich, I've got a location that I think will work for us.' So, in 1973 we opened Fritz That's It!, our second restaurant. The idea was, 'You've heard of the Ritz, now try the Fritz.' We sort of made fun of fancy restaurants, but who knew that, years later, I would actually own a series of upscale restaurants? Fred became our partner and the operator there.

Our third restaurant was The Great Gritzbe's Flying Food Show on Chestnut and State, and was our first restaurant that was actually located in downtown Chicago. Prior to us taking it over, this restaurant had failed five times. In fact, one of the people who had previously had a restaurant there was the famous Chef Jean Banchet. Around that time, everybody was trying to copy R.J. Grunts and its funny, eclectic menus, so with Gritzbe's, I decided to do something really different. I made the interior all grey, and instead of a salad bar, we had a cheese bar and a dessert bar. Gritzbe's, too, was pretty successful, lasting 10 years.

Next came Jonathan Livingston Seafood, located on Sheridan Road where we currently have our corporate headquarters. Sam Zell owned the building, and when one of his associates offered me the space, we took it for our next restaurant. We closed there after about eight or nine years because we lost the parking and soon realized that we wouldn't be able to offer enough parking to our customers. So we decided to make it into our offices and we grew into the space. Because Jonathan's was only a moderate success, we chose not to move it to another location. Also, I was tired of the name which, after awhile, I thought was silly. And, although I was through with that particular restaurant, I wasn't finished with the idea of having seafood restaurants.

After Jonathan's, we opened Lawrence of Oregano on Diversey Parkway where the New Capri, a popular Italian restaurant, had been. Bob Wattel, a college friend who is now a partner, and I loved the New Capri and went to it all the time. Jerry and I bought that building for Lawrence of Oregano, which, incidentally, was the last of our series of *goofy named* restaurants. There were certain things there that we duplicated years later at Maggiano's, so Lawrence of Oregano is where Maggiano's sort of got its start.

One Friday night in 1974, I was walking down the street near The Pump Room at the Ambassador East Hotel. I had never been in The Pump Room and wanted to take a look at it. At that time, we had four restaurants and each one had an hour and a half wait on Friday nights. I had heard my parents talk about The Pump Room and how they couldn't afford to have dinner there, so they once went there late one night to have dessert for a special occasion. I went in but I wasn't dressed properly to be seated, so Arturo Petterino, the maître d', said to me, 'I'm sorry, young man, but we have a dress code.' I said that I just wanted to see the restaurant, so he invited me in to just take a look around. I saw that the dining room was quite empty, with only six or seven tables seated, and I thought to myself, 'God, we have one hour plus waits at our restaurants, but this famous place isn't very busy. And it's a nice looking room—we should try to buy this restaurant.' So, I thanked Arturo and left. I realized that The Pump Room was in a good location in the high-end Gold Coast and that we should be able to do something *wild* with that space. I called Mark Friedman, the landlord at the Ambassador East, and left a message, telling him who I was. But he never returned my call. I then left him a second message, but still never heard back from him. So, I decided to forget about it since he didn't seem interested in me or my ideas.

About a year later, Sheldon Good, a well-known realtor and friend, called to say he had some interesting locations for restaurants that I might like to see. He told me about one location and I said no. He told me about

A wryly worded sign at the entrance to R.J. Grunts imparts the restaurant's significance as the cornerstone of a successful restaurant empire.

A Grunts lunch and dinner menu from 1971 (Eric Bronsky Collection).

another one, and I still said no. Then he said, 'Well, you're not going to be interested in the third one—it's The Pump Room.' My response was, 'I was very interested a year ago and had tried to contact Mark Friedman, but I don't think that guy wants me as a tenant because…' Sheldon said, 'Mark's a friend of mine, and I will get you guys together.' So, Jerry and I met with him, and I was real naïve. Mark asked me, 'So, what would you do with The Pump Room?' I said, 'I'll make it real special.' He asked, 'Like what?' Now, I had never seen the 21 Club in New York City, but I said, 'Well, it will be like the 21 Club.' He asked, 'Do you mean that it will look like the 21 Club?' I said, 'It's going to feel like the 21 Club.' I was making it up as I went along. A day or two later, Jerry and I went to see the 21 Club and I said, 'This isn't what I want!' So, Sheldon brokered the deal and we bought The Pump Room. It was losing money at that time and my lawyer convinced them that they would not only stop their losses, which were considerable, but they would get rent, which they weren't then getting. So, just by us buying it for a relatively small sum, they would stem their losses and turn it into a positive.

We owned The Pump Room for about 22 Club years until around 1988 Club. And, despite our early financial losses, it became very successful. I had several partners in that venture, including Cy Young Award winner Steve Stone, former Bears Quarterback Bobby Douglass, and my usual group of partners.

We didn't have a top chef at The Pump Room when we first started in 1977-1978. I had met Gabino Sotelino when he was the chef at Le Perroquet, which was considered one of the finest restaurants in the country. I loved Le Perroquet and what he was doing there. The food was simple, but sophisticated, and I asked Gabino, 'Why don't you come with me and become our chef?' But, it didn't feel right to him because Jovan Trboyevic, the owner, had promised him a partnership. So I said to him, 'If things don't work out, give me a call.' Within a year, I got a call from him, and he said, 'Hey, the partnership never happened, so let's talk.' I said to him, 'Well, I want you to come and help us organize The Pump Room, and serve the type of food that you do.'

Gabino helped me get The Pump Room under control. I knew he would be the right guy to do it, but he told me that The Pump Room really wasn't the type of restaurant he wanted to do for very long. He said, 'I want to be at a four-star, fine dining restaurant.' So, I said, 'Look, if you help me organize The Pump Room for the next year or two, I'll back you in that fine dining restaurant. So how's that?' He said, 'Great!' And that was it. We lost big money the first year of our operation in the range of $150,000. But I just took all the money from Grunts and put it into The

Pump Room, and I never thought of giving up on the restaurant. Gabino turned the place around, got it organized, and he was a great leader in the back of the house. I learned a lot working with him.

I constantly opened new restaurants, but the one after The Pump Room was Bones on Lincoln Avenue in Lincolnwood, where L. Woods is today. Bones got off to a slow start, but became very popular when Freddie Joast came in to help me out. I made a lot of mistakes with Bones by serving things that the clientele didn't understand or didn't want to understand. For example, we developed this special smoker for the ribs that encompassed an entire wall of the dining room for all the guests to see. Of course, if you smoke bacon or any meat over wood, it comes out sort of reddish. Well, I thought that the ribs were spectacular, but the clientele thought the ribs looked like underdone pink pork. So, that didn't work as I expected. Then, we brought in blue crabs from Baltimore, where my partner Steve Stone was pitching for the Orioles, but this didn't work because people said it was too messy and they hated it.

We were one of the first places in Chicago to put in a mesquite grill and, besides doing these really neat things, we were using this pit where we made barbecue ribs and brisket, as well as mesquite broiled fish. One of my partners, Charles Haskell, was a fisherman and a gourmand. He went to Seattle and, in 1975 or 1976, he discovered this fish cooked over wood and it was wonderful. He brought it back along with samples of the wood, and we built a special pit to cook the fish.

My friend, Billy Leach, who was a defensive back for U. of I., told me about this famous barbecue place in Champaign called Po' Boys. It was run by a guy named Arnie, and all the athletes used to go there for the great barbeque sauce and these sandwiches on white bread. My wife's family lived in Kankakee, which is about halfway between Chicago and downstate. So, my brother-in-law Mark would drive from Kankakee down to Arnie's, Arnie would put up the sauce for us, and then Mark would take it to Kankakee, where one of our guys would pick it up.

The brisket at Bones was cooked over wood and shaved real thin. So, we had what I thought were cool brisket sandwiches on white bread with Arnie's sauce, but people generally didn't get it. A few people who went to the University of Illinois and understood the concept got it, but the middle-age Jewish clientele just didn't get it. They wanted their brisket on Kaiser or onion rolls and not on white bread, and they wanted lemon meringue pie and not the chess pie. So, it seemed that nothing I offered to the Bones' customers caught on. Blue crabs didn't work, mesquite grilled fish didn't work, the ribs looked undercooked, the bread was wrong, and the chess pie was wrong. It seemed that it was one thing after another. As Larry Levy, a friend and fellow restaurateur, said, 'Rich, you wonder why customers aren't ordering a lot of fish—the place is called Bones!' I never had more people complain about anything that I had ever done, and while the restaurant was crowded for a while, we moved pretty quickly to change things.

Freddie Joast lived near the restaurant in Lincolnwood, and he said, 'Rich, I think what you are doing is very good. But, you really don't understand the clientele here.' He switched the menu, and, literally, within two to three months, the place was jumping.

I kept the restaurant menu the way that Freddie did it, and Bones stayed in business for about 23 years, after which time we decided to re-concept the restaurant. Our lease was up, and I wanted to stay there, so I decided that I was willing to take the gamble and make the change.

We changed the menu and renamed the restaurant L. Woods and we still got beat up bad. Our guests were very vocal and didn't like it because it involved making some changes, but eventually it worked out nicely, and now, L. Woods is very popular with a mixture of age groups.
As our business grew, many people would call me with new restaurant ideas. But Lettuce did not expand based on a specific plan and before I knew it, the number of restaurants grew to eight.

My next restaurant was Ambria in 1980, located in the Belden-Stratford Hotel in Lincoln Park. Ambria was the first real, fine dining restaurant that we ever did, although The Pump Room was in that style. We did a lot of planning and working on this one. I went to France for the first time, traveling with my wife and Gabino Sotelino. We spent four weeks there, eating and seeing some of the things that he envisioned for the restaurant.
We came back home and found a wonderful location, and I said, 'Let's go.'

Ambria really took off, and it was a very important and popular restaurant in Chicago. I remember working there for about six months, so it was a great way for me to learn fine dining and a whole different way of service. For me it was a special experience and I learned a lot. We were very successful with Ambria for 20-some years, and then we replaced it with L20.

My partner, Gabino, is no longer cooking. We had opened a number of other restaurants together, and he was living in Spain for part of the year, Chicago for part of the year, and in Las Vegas for part of the year. We opened a couple of restaurants in Vegas that were very successful, and he decided to live in Vegas. Without Gabino in Chicago, Ambria didn't have the same day-to-day attention and I honestly felt that the restaurant at that point was good, but not great. It was making a little money, but I didn't feel good about it. I wanted to do one more four-star type restaurant, and I wanted it to be a seafood restaurant. So it was Ambria, Everest, Tru, and then L2o, a three-star Michelin restaurant. I had wanted to do a seafood restaurant for the longest time and had wanted to call it 'One if by Land, Two if by Sea,' but that name was taken. So we named it L2O for 'Lakes, Seas, Oceans.'

From 1980 until now, I have been doing high-end food, beginning at The Pump Room and Ambria, and I feel good about it. It was a great experience. I think that it got me out of that image that this guy can just do hamburger-type things. And I like being able to go from fast food, like an M Burger, to a four-star cuisine. It feels right for me. I think that my own personal growth is reflected in how I paint. In fact, learning about food in a different way has been a great growing experience.

Un Grand Café, which is now Mon Ami Gabi, was an outgrowth of the employee meals at Ambria. I loved the staff meals there and thought, 'Wow, we ought to do a restaurant utilizing this type of rustic French bistro food.' There had been a restaurant in that location called The Tree House, owned by Al Farber and his son. The meals that they used to make at Ambria for the back of the house and front of the house staff were so good that we created Un Grand Café.

Our partners have five-year plans, but I say to them, 'Don't even tell me about it. As long as you are willing to change every day, I am willing to live with you guys having a five-year plan.' With me, it's a matter of, 'I will know what's right when I get there' and that is how I work. My way of developing restaurants is to have what I would call "tunnel vision," meaning that I always remain very focused on what I am doing at any given time.

We have had opportunities to franchise from early on, like the Corner Bakery, but I have never built more than 10 of anything. During our second year in business, Ann Landers' husband, Jules Lederer, came in to Grunts and loved it. He wanted to know who the owner was, and he approached me with an idea. At the time, he was involved in a rental car business through-out Europe. He said, 'I can just sense these things. You have got something so unique and so wonderful that I could take it all over Europe and we could take it all over the United States.' And he was not the first person who had approached me and said that we could take this thing and make it big. Ironically, it was quite funny to Jerry and me because we said, 'No, we don't want to do that. We have one Grunts, and we're keeping it like this.'

So, I have never had a goal of being the biggest. We've grown, and I sort of think of the restaurants as my 'kids' and I don't like selling the 'kids.' Will I sell any of my restaurant business? Yeah. You want to know why we sold Maggiano's and the Corner Bakery? It's because my partners wanted to do it. I wouldn't have done it; I would have kept them. I'll bet you that if I had kept them, we would probably have only 10 Maggiano's now and not 50-plus, and we would only have 12 Corner Bakeries and not 100 or 110.

In terms of the success of Wildfire, what we tried to do there was set the foundation for it as a moderately priced steakhouse. When we created it about 16 years ago, moderately priced steakhouses were costing the diner $40 a person, and the expensive ones were $50. We said that we wanted to open a $25-$28 dining experience. So we said, let's make it opulent enough so that you are getting a real value even though you are not paying as much, and that was the idea. It is simple food done well and moderately priced. It caught on, and they do extremely well. This is a steakhouse, but not with a limited menu because we expanded it and it worked.

I think that I am part artist and part businessman. I never had the goal of being the richest, the biggest, or the most well-known. I tell our publicity people that it doesn't matter to me if they ever mention me in the restaurant promotional materials. It's just not what interests me. I am happy to be a spokesperson for the company if it helps Lettuce, but they don't need to mention me. Now I concentrate more on the creative aspects of the business, while Kevin Brown, our president and CEO, focuses on the day-to-day business side. I do a lot of talking about our culture. Kevin and I don't overlap in our functions, and we've got people who do what they do well. I am a very happy guy who is creating behind the scenes, making sure that these restaurants are right and making sure that the Lettuce culture is intact."

Kevin J. Brown, President and Chief Executive Officer, Lettuce Entertain You Enterprises Inc.: "Clearly a Chicago classic restaurant since it opened in 1971, and one that is still is very close to my heart, is R.J. Grunts. I love it there, and not only because I began my LEYE career at that restaurant. When I first came to town, I was at a meeting at The Pump Room with Rich Melman and one of his partners, Charles Haskell, along with another guy who, like me, was new to LEYE. We met them at that restaurant and Rich said to my friend, Tim Jenkins, that he wanted Tim to go work at Grunts while I should begin at The Great Gritzbe's Flying Food Show. Rich asked us, 'Is that okay?' I looked down and said, 'If it doesn't matter to anybody, I would prefer to go to Grunts.' Talk about a good career move. I not only love what R.J. Grunts means to us, but also the fact that it has become a Chicago icon. As for Gritzbe's, it closed for a number of reasons, including the fact that I think it didn't have the LEYE identity in the same way as Grunts.

I consider Shaw's Crab House to be a classic seafood restaurant. I am probably a bit biased in my opinion because the place is actually named for

R. J. Grunts' main dining room as it appeared in 2011 was virtually unchanged from its 1971 appearance (Eric Bronsky photo).

Gritzbe's featured an award-winning interior design by artists Karen and Tony Barone. Colors were predominantly gray; the bar area featured a cheese bar and a multilevel sculpted seating area (photo by Alexandre Georges).

An early Gritzbe's menu.

A wine list from Fritz That's It!, which opened in 1973.

The backside of a Lawrence of Oregano menu typifies the offbeat humor that made the early LEYE restaurants hip and popular (courtesy of Herb Russel).

The Great Gritzbe's FLYING FOOD SHOW

Lettuce Entertain You Enterprises

Creators of
R.J. Grunts,
Fritz Thats It!,
The Great Gritzbes Flying Food Sh...
Jonathan Livingston Sea...
...and opening late...
The D...

LEYE's talented and creative staff brought one original restaurant concept after another to success.

Kevin Brown opened Shaw's Crab House for LEYE in 1984, Gabino Sotelino opened Café Ba-Ba-Reeba!, Chicago's first Spanish tapas restaurant, in 1986, and the first of several Wildfire restaurants opened on Erie Street in 1995 (Eric Bronsky photos).

my wife's maiden name. Shaw's took a lot of chances with its location and size, and we always focused on the quality of the food along with a simpler preparation. Other LEYE classic restaurants should include Un Grand Café/Mon Ami Gabi. Mon Ami Gabi has become as close to a neighborhood bistro as there is in America. It is a French restaurant that is a favorite of regular diners and is located in a perfect neighborhood where people use it as their club.

Ambria was clearly a Chicago classic restaurant. Rich opened it in order to change the face of fine dining in Chicago, and I think that what Rich and Gabino Sotelino did was to introduce elegant, fine food along with a sense of humor. As a result, they took some of the "haute" out of haute dining. It was high cuisine, but not high attitude. The servers at Ambria were confident but they had a sense of humor, were approachable, and they talked to people. It wasn't "I'm more important than you," but, instead, "you can talk to us and we won't be snobbish." I know what a passion Ambria was for Rich, and it elevated the entire organization's taste level and convinced everyone at LEYE that we could go higher. When we were getting ready to open Ambria, I would go in and see Gabino preparing the restaurant. I had the privilege to watch how the kitchen got built and the way he made the food, and I was really fascinated.

The Pump Room, which Rich owned by the time I got to Chicago, was a very special place. In fact, it was a magical, exciting and glittery night when we could use our management cards to go there (a discount or a free meal, once a month). I especially remember the spinach salad and the soufflés they served there. In late May 1978, Rich contacted me because the general manager of The Pump Room had called R.J. Grunts and said, 'I need Kevin to be a manager at The Pump Room since the number two manager is leaving.' I went there and it was wonderful, and although I loved Booth One, what I really loved was the big kitchen and the great chefs."

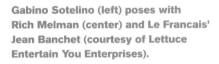

Gabino Sotelino (left) poses with Rich Melman (center) and Le Francais' Jean Banchet (courtesy of Lettuce Entertain You Enterprises).

It was a tradition for VIPs dining at The Pump Room to be seated in Booth One. Celebrity sightings over the years included Comedians Bud Abbott and Lou Costello.

Chicago sports impresarios George Halas and Bill Veeck, with Bobby Douglass (standing).

Film critic Roger Ebert with
actor John Belushi

Playboy founder Hugh Hefner with singer
Nancy Sinatra and *Chicago Sun-Times*
columnist Irv Kupcinet (all photos courtesy
of Lettuce Entertain You Enterprises).

Bob Darling, Mercer Island, WA: "When I was a freshman in college, my sister, who had already graduated from college, was working and she invited me to lunch at The Pump Room. I ordered the half cantaloupe filled with their world-famous shrimp salad. I'll never forget it because I thought to myself, 'Does life get any better than this?'"

Dick Kuhlman, Arlington, TX: "The Pump Room is a place I'd heard of but had never been to before. One day, my boss took me to lunch there and I had heard stories that there were always celebrities dining at the restaurant. Sure enough, there was the actor Van Johnson having lunch with friends and also, William Kunstler, the famed attorney for the notorious Chicago 7 Conspiracy Trial. I was impressed."

Phil Shapiro: "For our first wedding anniversary, we went to The Pump Room at the Ambassador Hotel. Now, it may sound silly today, but I will never forget asking for and having a telephone brought to our table and it being plugged it in. I used it to call my grandmother to tell her I was at The Pump Room at the Ambassador. I remember the wallpaper was like covered with velvet and everything was just so expensive. I think I'm still paying for it, but it was such a grown-up place to go. And here I was, in the Secret Service, probably making 12 cents an hour. I remember my wife asking me not to wear my gun because it made my suit not hang right. It bothered me all night that I wasn't armed. But, it was such a classy place and I had been forewarned that if there were two forks on the table, not to send one back. Everybody was so well dressed. Some people were even in tuxedos."

Joe Mantegna: "Peter Falk and I were appearing in *Glengarry Glen Ross* on tour in Chicago and we were both staying at the Ambassador West. We decided to go over to The Pump Room at the Ambassador East for a late dinner. We walked in and it was very dark—late, about 10:30. The maître d' could barely see us, because as I said, it's kind of dark. So the maître d' says, 'Can I help you?' So, I said, 'Yeah, the two of us would like to get some dinner.' And he looked at me and said, 'You're not wearing a jacket. This is The Pump Room and you can't come in here without a jacket.' 'Oh, we've just come from appearing in the play.' And he said, 'I'm sorry, but that's our policy. You've got to have a jacket.' So, now I turned and revealed Peter standing behind me and said, 'Peter, we can't go in. We've got to have jackets.' So, now the maître d' sees him and says, 'Peter Falk! Oh my God! Peter Falk!' Next thing you know, he's almost

A Pump Room waiter proffers a flaming sword to entertainer Eddie Fisher (courtesy of Lettuce Entertain You Enterprises).

dragging us into the restaurant and we're in Booth One. So, I got an early taste of the power of celebrity from Peter Falk. He knew it all along and said to the maître d' in that gravely voice, 'How ya' doin'? How ya' doin'?' That was it...we were in."

Jerrod and RJ Melman, owners of Hub 51 and Paris Club:

Jerrod: "RJ and I talk all day, every day, and we are always bouncing ideas off of each other. It was a dynamic that I think we both saw, and although we didn't say it out loud, within that first month of working together we wanted to do something as a team, begin planning a project, and just list ideas for restaurants. Up to that point we had worked in restaurants where we had a lot of pride in them but nothing that felt like it was what each of us wanted or worth pouring our souls into. I think that my dad would say about Grunts that he used every good idea he ever had and anything he ever wanted to try in one restaurant. Hub 51 was that experience for us and it allowed us to try out all of our ideas about restaurants.

Today, Hub is probably all we had envisioned it to be and more, although it would be fair to say that we had unclear images of the final result. RJ and I would say to each other that our restaurant should look open, big, raw, and industrial. But RJ thought the servers should wear Nike Shox, and they don't. We actually had a meeting with Nike and they could not have been less interested in our staff wearing Shox. However, when we met with the people who made Vans, they were really psyched about our concept and were willing to give us all the pairs of shoes we wanted for our staff. In our minds, Hub 51 was going to be a California-infused restaurant, and Vans is a California company."

RJ: "Hub 51 opened in 2008 and the creation of our menu was very methodical. We believe that today it has become an 'in-place' for our generation. We named it Hub after its location on Hubbard Street and 51 for the actual address, but we wanted it to be an emotional hub for this area of the city. Chris Mears has been our partner at that restaurant and has been a wonderful mentor to us."

Jerrod: "Chris pushed us in a lot of ways, and differently than Dad could do because sometimes it is too familiar when it is your dad, even though he did provide us with continuous and constructive input. Sometimes Dad would leave us alone, and sometimes he would really be an active participant in the decision-making process. I have to imagine that it is somewhat like

Hub 51 and Paris Club are next-door neighbors (Eric Bronsky photos).

129

having a grandkid because when he thought we were doing things right, he would get excited. On the other hand, when he thought that we were doing things wrong he was not the type of person who could sit idly by and watch without expressing his opinion."

RJ: "I should note that we don't always agree with him, but sometimes we try out his ideas just to see how they work. But sometimes those ideas don't work, although I have to admit that it is more annoying when he is right."

While Melman and his LEYE restaurants were first being introduced to a young clientele in the '70s, another restaurateur, Lawrence Levy, with his partners, was opening a new group of creative and fun restaurants, along with some fine dining establishments that included Spiaggia, Café Spiaggia, Chestnut Street Grill, D.B. Kaplan's, Jake Melnick's Corner Tap, and Bistro 110. The main difference in Levy's growth came in the 1980s when he and his company made the decision to go in a different direction than Melman. Their new business model focused on selling high quality food to the premier, skybox clients along with the general public at America's sports ventures. Today, Levy Restaurants provides food service to more than 40 sports teams and stadiums around the country, and the Levy name, like the Melman name, has come to stand for excellence, quality, creativity, and fun in the dining experience.

Lawrence F. Levy, Chairman, Levy Restaurants: "I started in the restaurant business at 32 with my brother Mark, who was 30. Our first restaurant in Chicago was D.B. Kaplan's, located in Water Tower Place on the seventh floor. Admittedly we made the big mistake of having the restaurant situated on the seventh floor when, at that time, there were no other restaurants above the second floor in Chicago. In addition, most of the seventh floor had nothing but empty spaces at the time we opened. Luckily D.B. Kaplan's became insanely popular very quickly. A travel pattern developed in the building in which visitors to Water Tower Place, at the time Chicago's top tourist attraction, would take the building's beautiful glass elevators to the seventh floor and then use the escalators on their way down back to the lower floors while doing shopping. D.B. Kaplan's became the first stop. In addition to our questionable location on the seventh floor of Water Tower Place, we made some other 'beginners' mistakes, including having 250 items on the menu. The trick was that it was permutations and combinations of many of the same Jewish delicacies. My mother Eadie, who has always been a very important person in our company, came up from St. Louis to help my brother and me because the food when we opened wasn't as good as hers.

We still give an Eadie Award each year to someone special at Levy Restaurants as our version of the Oscar. A year later, my mother permanently moved from St. Louis to Chicago to make sure the food was authentic and has been our 'company mom' and inspired provider of superb recipes ever since and our MVP and keeper of the family culture in the company.

The original chef at D.B, Kaplan's thought we were 'rubes.' One day my brother Mark said to him, 'You're never here during the day. Why is that?' He told Mark that chefs work at night but my brother responded, 'Look, if you ever get hit by a truck, I want to know how to make these dishes.' So, late one night, Mark came to the restaurant and discovered that the chef hadn't shown up. Well, the chef never showed up again and when we opened his locker we found the answer: he had a book called Famous Jewish Recipes, which he had by his side to make the Jewish dishes at the restaurant. The book was marked down many times on the cover from $19.99 to $1! Today the company has revenue close to one billion dollars and I often think back to our origins and that it all started with that $1 discounted book of recipes.

Two years after opening D.B. Kaplan's in Water Tower Place, we opened the Chestnut Street Grill, Hillary's, and Eaternity. Chestnut Street Grill was located where Mity Nice Grill is located today on the mezzanine and, on the sixth level, we also operated Dos Hermanos, a Mexican restaurant. The reason that we eventually closed those restaurants at the end of their leases was because Water Tower Place had gone through changes in its traffic counts and demographics. When Water Tower Place first opened, it was the center of the universe on North Michigan Avenue and in Chicago. Many Chicagoans and visitors alike would go there to hang out. It became a city unto itself because it was a day and nighttime place that had movie theaters and a theater for live plays. Chestnut Street Grill, in my opinion, was the best fish restaurant in Chicago, and Hillary's looked like a restaurant/bar that Ralph Lauren designed. Both were wildly successful. However, when more stores and malls opened on North Michigan Avenue, Water Tower Place became just another place and, as a result, we lost our premium. With our restaurant sales declining, we just decided to refocus our business. Our other restaurants in Chicago have included Spiaggia, Café Spiaggia, Bistro 110, and Jake Melnick's Corner Tap. As for Bistro 110, located on Pearson Street just west of Michigan Avenue, it had been called Don Roth's Blackhawk on Pearson in an attempt to continue Don Roth's success of his famous Loop restaurant. Because the place wasn't doing as well as hoped and only had $1 million in sales, Don's son Doug came to us with a partnership proposal to work with us to convert it into a bistro, which became Bistro 110. We added an outside covered eating area like in Paris, and it was the first of those in Chicago. Basically, we came up with a mythology that it was a little Parisian zinc bar run by a husband and wife. It became so popular that we eventually expanded it into bigger rooms.

Another part of the mythology of Bistro 110 was that the art in the restaurant was traded for food by the struggling artists who later became famous. So, we had a lot of art work there and we created an environment at Bistro 110 that looked like it was a late 19th century iconic Parisian bistro. It has been a very successful restaurant for more than 20 years. Doug Roth got tired of it about ten years ago and asked us if we would buy him out and we agreed. We continued to attract both local diners and out of town visitors. Our policy is that we try to locate our restaurants where visitors might come, but we do not own strictly neighborhood restaurants.

In August of 2011, after 23 years, we closed Bistro 110. We are opening a very special Italian restaurant in the location in October 2011 headed by Spiaggia's illustrious chef, Tony Mantuano, who won the prestigious James Beard Award for best Chef in the Midwest.

In my opinion, the most perfect restaurant we ever created is Spiaggia and its 'little sister' Café Spiaggia in 1983, located at 980 North Michigan Avenue. They were led at the outset by Chef Tony Mantuano. I was the developer of One Magnificent Mile, the 1-million-square-foot building where Spiaggia is located and where 181 condominiums and 400,000 square feet of office tenants reside.

As background, in the 1960s, there was a fire on that block that burned down a major building on half of the block at Oak Street and Michigan Avenue. The owners of the block called me because they wanted me to build an office building at another location they owned. I asked if they would sell the property at Michigan Avenue and Oak Street, and their response was that if anyone was stupid enough to pay $8.5 million, they would sell the entire block to me. I asked, 'Can I give you $50,000 as an option and then have 18 months to try to create a mixed use zoning like the John Hancock Building and Water Tower Place?' The owners said yes to my offer. I borrowed $50,000 for the down payment and began to design the building under the guidance of Bruce Graham, the chief designer for Skidmore, Owings & Merrill. Bruce also designed the Hancock Building and Sears Tower.

I actually had envisioned what Spiaggia would look like before we even broke ground, including the 33-foot ceiling and tiered seating of the restaurant facing Lake Michigan. I have always loved Italian food while never being a particular fan of classic French food, the more likely cuisine for an iconic high-end restaurant in the early '80s. Italian food, with its big powerful flavors and fabulous ingredients, always attracted me. In fact, I love Italian people, Italy with Mark and our wives to see Tony and check on his progress.

culture, clothes, art, and films. In order to complete the restaurant, I had to find $1.5 million, which I did not have. I spent the construction period of the building scared to death because two months after I commenced the construction of One Magnificent Mile in 1980, the prime interest rate shot up to 20 percent.

One day, as I was struggling to find the capital to build Spiaggia, I received a serendipitous call from a friend who said she met a woman who had recently moved to Chicago, had just finished her degree at the Kellogg School at Northwestern, and who was currently working at Foote, Cone & Belding. She was from a very important Wisconsin family and was looking to invest in a restaurant. Her father, the patriarch of the family, gave each child a generous amount of money that had to be invested in a risky venture because he wanted each of his children to learn how to fend for themselves. Of course, restaurants are the riskiest of investments. It turned out to be Helen Johnson from the S.C. Johnson family. The family became equal partners with us in Spiaggia and Café Spiaggia, and a year later, our partnership added the Private Dining Rooms of Spiaggia. The restaurants were from the outset a big success and the Johnsons were world- class partners. We had board of directors meetings twice a year, one in Racine, Wisconsin and one in Chicago at Spiaggia. Sam Johnson, then the patriarch of this wonderful family, said to me, 'We really like your whole business. Would you trade us our 50 percent in Spiaggia for a percentage of your entire company?' They ended up owning a small percentage of Levy Restaurants and making a fabulous investment that worked out well for everyone.

Spiaggia had the first log burning oven ever permitted to be built in a Chicago highrise. It was a homemade enclosed wood burning stove that heated to 1,000 degrees. To comply with Chicago building code, we had to find a way to cool the oven down before the heat rose to the next floor. We had an equipment designer who invented a way to pipe the smoke back and forth until it cooled down. The wonderful accident that happened was that the food got a perfect smoky flavor. We later built the same oven at many stadiums, as well as at Walt Disney World and Bistro 110.

Spiaggia received spectacular reviews and finally people took Mark and me seriously as restaurateurs and culinarians. Spiaggia became our signature restaurant. Prior to Spiaggia, the food press thought we were only entrepreneurs who were opening restaurants, and we took it quite personally. We have always been passionate about hospitality, food, and wine.

I actually selected the materials for the exterior of One Magnificent Mile in Carrara, Italy and sent Tony Mantuano to Italy to work for a full year learning Italian cooking at the very best restaurants in Italy. Then I went to We also selected many of the materials that are still used today in the restaurant and throughout the building.

Since 1984, we have continuously operated at another restaurant location at Wabash and Superior, previously the location for Randall's Ribhouse for 12 years and the Blackhawk Lodge for nine years. We then changed it to Jake Melnick's Corner Tap, a place that is actually named for our driver of 30 years, a real Chicago character named James 'Jake' Melnick. It has always done very well, is a classic Chicago sports bar serving wonderful, comfort food, and is now at its business peak. Jake Melnick's is hugely busy any time there is a big sporting event as it provides diners with 25 televisions and is just a fun place. Although it is a great location today, that was not always the case because the blocks west of North Michigan Avenue 25 years ago did not attract many people. Jake's has the floor that was used at Blackhawk Lodge, which includes 100-year-old floorboards brought from South Carolina. The entire restaurant has a great weathered patina.

By far the most important decision we ever made was to continue to make our restaurants phenomenal but not to open many more. Instead, we decided that Levy Restaurants would concentrate on our sports and entertainment catering business, which started at Chicago's first skyboxes at the old Comiskey Park in 1982. We thought that the United States was going to have a wave of new stadiums and arenas, and that Europe and Asia would eventually follow. We surveyed the competition, which was comprised of huge corporations with little culinary and service excellence, and decided that we could be a very serious player in sports foodservice. It turned out that, if the food looked good, tasted good, and was served by nice people (Chicago hospitality), then our guests would eat and drink far more than the competition's food per capita. We also discovered that we could afford to pay more to the sports teams than our competition and that the only way the large companies could compete with us was to make outrageously bad business deals for themselves. As a result, three of the largest competitors went bankrupt.

Today, Levy Restaurants is the market leader in fine dining foodservice for sports stadiums across North America, including 20 of the 30 NBA venues and large percentages of football, baseball, hockey, and horse racing venues. The 'Levy Difference' is that we serve the highest restaurant quality food in sports venues. In other words, we are a restaurant company operating in sports with the point of view of a 'street' restaurateur. If you get a hot dog, I guarantee that it is hotter with a fresher bun and better mustard. While everybody talks about the great restaurateurs, I do not think any of them ever built such a successful food business using Chicago recipes combined with Chicago style hospitality."

The Levys' first restaurant was D.B. Kaplan's, a Jewish deli which opened on the seventh floor of Water Tower Place in 1978. Its menu featured a long list of sandwiches, most with wacky names.

FRESH FEATURES

All sandwiches from #1 thru #148 include pickle and your choice of potato salad, cole slaw or potato chips.

1. **THE CALIFORNIAN**—Hot, open faced sandwich of melted monterey jack and cheddar cheese over turkey, sliced tomatoes, avocados, and toasted almonds on wheat toast. $4.95
2. **SPROUTS OF THIS WORLD**—Plain cream cheese, sliced cucumber, sliced black olives and alfalfa sprouts, served cold on a CROISSANT. $4.50
3. **PERKY TURKEY**—Turkey salad mixed with crushed pineapple, topped with leaf lettuce and served cold on a CROISSANT. $4.95
4. **PITA YOUR HEART OUT**—Pita bread stuffed with artichoke hearts, alfalfa sprouts, black olives, sliced tomato and bermuda onions. Dressed with vinaigrette. $4.95
5. **THREE'S A CROWD**—Swiss, herkimer cheddar and muenster cheeses, shredded lettuce and tomato slices with M&M on french bread. Great cold, but even better HOT! $4.95
6. **AVA-CADA DEAL FOR YOU?**—Avocado, tomato slices, lettuce, and monterey jack cheese on wheat bread. $4.95

TRIPLE DECKERS FOR BIG FRESSERS —

7. **A BRISKET, A BASKET**—Better not be bashful! Layers of beef brisket, beef tongue, breast of turkey and Vienna corned beef . . . add monterey jack and herkimer cheddar cheeses with lots of shredded lettuce, bermuda onion and tomato slices on Rosen's jewish cholly. Marvelous! $7.50
8. **TONGUE FU**—Beef tongue, pepperbeef and corned beef, with swiss cheese and dusseldorf mustard on black bread served HOT! $5.50
9. **STUDS TURKEY**—Breast of turkey, all beef tongue and canadian style bacon mounded upon shredded lettuce and whole cranberry sauce served HOT on french bread. $5.50
10. **SGT. PEPPER'S LONELY**—Vienna pepperbeef, baked ham, hickory smoked bacon, swiss cheese, bermuda onions and mayo served HOT on an onion roll. $5.50
11. **THE AFFAIR**—Vienna corned beef, roast beef, cole

SANDWICHES
DELI FAVORITES

Z-Z-Z-Zoup

BREADLESS BEAUTIE

79. **BERMUDA SCHWARTZ**—Roast beef, shredded lettuce, bermuda onion, tomato slices and mayo between slices of muenster cheese (no bread). $4
80. **LIVERS AND OTHER STRANGERS** — Vienna corned beef, chopped liver, bermuda onions, tomato slices, M&M between slices of monterey jack cheese (no bread). $4
81. **FOWL PLAY**—Breast of turkey, shredded lettuce, tomato slices, and russian dressing between slices of swiss cheese (no bread). $4
82. **THE BREADLESS HORSEMAN** — Danish ham, shredded lettuce, tomato, dusseldorf mustard between slices of colby longhorn cheese (no bread). $4
83. **WHOLE EARTH**—Avocado slices, sliced tomato, alfalfa sprouts, leaf lettuce, served between slices of swiss cheese. Served with yogurt cucumber dressing (no bread). $4
84. **ALFALFA OMEGA**—Hickory smoked bacon, sliced mushrooms, sliced tomatoes, alfalfa sprouts, served hot between slices of swiss cheese (no bread). $4

OPEN FACED

85. **LITTLE MISS MUFFIN**—White meat tuna salad, sliced tomato, and cheddar cheese on a toasted English muffin, served hot. $4
86. **BIG BEN**—Breast of turkey, hickory smoked bacon, shredded lettuce, tomato slices and Russian dressing with swiss cheese on a toasted English muffin, served hot. $4
87. **ON TOP OF OLD SMOKEY**—Homemade turkey salad, sliced tomatoes and smoked cheddar cheese served on a toasted English muffin. $4
88. **HAM-LET**—Danish ham, alfalfa sprouts, artichoke hearts with vinegar and oil dressing. Served on a toasted English muffin. A-Classic! $4

WITH A TOUCH OF THE SEA

89. **LOX, STOCK AND BAGEL**—Nova Scotia lox, canadian bacon, chive cream cheese and tomato slices served open faced on a toasted bagel. $5
90. **THE NAVEL BATTLE**—Belly lox, white fish caviar and cream cheese with chives served open faced on black bread. $5

Chef Tony Mantuano, Chef/Partner, Spiaggia: "My fiancé, Cathy Mantuano, had moved to Chicago with me from Milwaukee. She was waiting tables at the Chestnut Street Grill in Water Tower where she would work during lunch, and it seemed that every day she would wait on Larry and Mark Levy. They were talking about the block where Spiaggia is located today (One Magnificent Mile), and were discussing the fact that they were going to be developing that building. Their goal was to open the best Italian restaurant in the city, if not the country. Cathy said to Larry, 'You should meet my fiancé.' As it turned out, that was how I connected with Larry. We sat down, talked about my skills and his goals for the restaurant, and he invited me to his house in Lincoln Park in order to cook a meal for him. After dinner, Larry said to me, 'You know, it's really delicious.' Everyone at that meal was a well-known Chicagoan. A while later, we cooked a second meal at the Levy's, and Larry said to me, 'Okay, the job is yours at my new restaurant, but we are not going to open for a year and a half. I have established business connections in Italy in order to buy marble and granite for my new building. Why don't you and Cathy go work in Italy, you in the kitchen and she in the front of the house? I will take care of all your expenses while you are away, so go live there for a year and work,' and that is exactly what we did. We worked in Italy for a year, and when we returned to Chicago, we did a sort of after-education dinner back at Larry's house, with the same group of dining guests, and I had a lot of fun.

That second dinner happened in 1984, and we opened Spiaggia on Friday, April 13, 1984. Everyone said that it was bad luck to open on that date, but we weren't concerned because in Italy the number 13 brings Italians luck and is like our number 7 here. I just thought that it was a good day to open.

The first year we were in business, it seemed that every Hollywood star and local politician was checking us out because we were a different type of restaurant. We have continued to attract the stars and politicians, as well as local diners, over the past 25 years, and when they come to Chicago or work here, they make certain to eat at Spiaggia. I would compare our success in many ways to that experienced by The Pump Room in the '40s and '50s. I think that we have achieved that status despite the fact that many restaurant connoisseurs would share with me their advice and opinions about what we were doing with our food. In fact, there was one particular restaurant owner who asked me to sit down right after we first opened, and he said, 'Everything is great, but kid, you're never going to make it if you don't put a meatball on the menu.' Despite his advice, we never have served meatballs and, ironically, I think that his place is no longer in business. In 1984, our food was classified as northern Italian. That distinguished us from the red sauce-meatball places found in the Italian neighborhoods. Now, that term has become sort of obsolete because every city and every region in Italy, all the way down to Sicily, has this style of restaurant that did not exist in 1984. And the 'Ferrari' type of restaurant is now available in every major city and major region in Italy. The accepted term is definitely 'modern Italian' even though that might scare some people.

We get our inspiration from all over Italy, and one of the reasons why Spiaggia has been so successful is that we try not to filter our menu through American tastes or emulate other Italian restaurants in this country, and it means that we go right to the source. While I was in Italy, I worked at Del Pescatore, one of the model restaurants in that country which has been there forever and is now on its second family generation. It's the restaurant to me that shows the example of hospitality and excellence and respect to the ingredients of that region and it is just an elegant place. When Cathy and I were working in Italy at Del Pescatore, Nadia and Antonio Santini were in charge. Nadia was pregnant when we were there and now their children are involved in operating the restaurant. Sara Gruenberg is our executive chef at Spiaggia, and when I first brought her on board, I sent her to Del Pescatore to work, learn, and absorb the Italian culture. Now she loves Italy, even though she is a German Texan, but wishes she was Italian and goes back there all the time. That helps to maintain our connection to Italy.

It is my personal opinion that no other Italian restaurant in Chicago compares to Spiaggia with our food, setting, and the ambience of our place. I am convinced that celebrities stop here because this is a grand space and a great place where one can dine while, at the same time, look out over the Magnificent Mile, Lake Shore Drive, and the lakefront. While I think that we have the premier Italian restaurant in town, it has been confirmed by the fact that restaurant critics continue to praise us and we are the only Italian restaurant that receives four stars from *Chicago Magazine, Chicago Tribune* and *Chicago Sun-Times*. In addition, I won a James Beard Award-Midwest in 2005, Spiaggia has been nominated ten times either for Outstanding Restaurant in America or Outstanding Service in America, and we have one star from Michelin (although we would like to have another star).

One of the things which is the hallmark of what we do and has been that way since we opened in 1984 is that we make all of our pastas in-house. They are all handcrafted, every single day, which can mean that between the main restaurant, the Café, and the Private Dining Rooms upstairs, we are making 15 different pastas every day. In fact, we have a full-time pasta-making team of three people who come in to the restaurant at 8 a.m. and leave at 4 p.m. each day.

Spiaggia, Levy's magnificent flagship restaurant, introduced Chicago to contemporary Italian cuisine in 1984 (courtesy of Lawrence Levy).

The second special thing here is our wood-burning oven. We have one here, one in the Café, and one in the Private Dining Rooms, and that is a flavor you can't duplicate. That wood, high heat, and smokiness adds our special flavors, and it is just a huge boost for us. We also have a great repeat clientele and I appreciate that they want to see me each time they come here. The Café is more of a local restaurant, so I know a lot of people who are in the Café every single night…a lot of regulars, while the Private Dining Rooms are used for special occasions.

We are in our 27th year, and we probably had our best year ever in 2010, in the middle of the crazy economic times. I don't physically cook every single dish in this restaurant anymore, but on *Top Chef Masters*, I had to do everything from cleaning the shrimp to making my own pasta and sometimes for up to 100 people. It was physically and emotionally draining, but I made a lot of good friends on the show, and, now, when I walk through the Dining Room or the Café, three or four people want to take their picture with me and that never happened before. So, *Top Chef Masters* is a powerful brand.

As for where Spiaggia is going and where restaurants are going in Chicago, I think that the answer you will get from most people is that you can't easily do high-end dining anymore in Chicago. You have to be casual or affordable, and, that is probably true if you are opening today. But it doesn't mean there isn't room in a major, world-class city like Chicago where people travel from all parts of the globe for the creation of a high-end restaurant. You still have to have that special place, and I would like Spiaggia to stay as one of the city's special places. I don't want to say that five years from now someone begins to compare us to a restaurant from the past. The key is bringing in new talent, so someone like Sara, who is 29 years old and who loves Italy, will continue to be a big part of what happens here. There is also no simple answer to the question of where the new chefs are being trained. It has to do with the person. I never went to culinary school, but Sara did, so, you just have to find that right person who loves Italian food. I don't want someone to work here if they don't love Italy and Italian culture. All of us love Italy, and that is what we look for: we look for people who want to cook Italian, who want to be Italian, who want to live Italian."

In addition to the Melman and Levy restaurants, from 1970 until the present, Chicago has enjoyed a wide variety of fine, even classic, dining that was typified by The Bakery, created by the late chef/owner Chef Louis Szathmary, The Bakery, owned and operated by Szathmary, was on Lincoln Avenue in the Lincoln Park neighborhood from 1962 until 1989 and was one of the most popular restaurants in Chicago during those years. Diners always remember the popular chef/owner greeting them as he moved among the tables, talking about his food and encouraging purchases of his cookbook.

Among his famous dishes were beef Wellington, beef Stroganoff, and roasted duckling covered in cherry sauce. It was also an establishment that did not serve liquor, but instead was BYOB.

Kevin J. Brown: "I came to Chicago in 1977, and in the fall of that year, I met some college friends and we went to eat at the famous Bakery on Lincoln Avenue. My first impression was that it was a little cathedral-like, which meant that you knew you were walking into someplace special. It looked like a bookstore, and the dining room was very proper and together, and diners had to bring their own wine for dinner. So, we brought something that said Bordeaux on it and felt pretty good about the wine selection even though we didn't spend a lot of money on the bottle. I remember asking the waiter for more pate, which he grudgingly brought to our table. I ordered their beef Wellington en croûte and I was smitten, loved the Bakery, and I just thought that it was wonderful dining. At 22 years old, you don't do a lot of dining at fancy restaurants, but I had heard so much about The Bakery that I had to experience the place for myself. Chef Louis Szathmary, the chef/owner, was at the restaurant that night and he came by the table. I told him that I was working for Lettuce Entertain You and R.J. Grunts, and he said to me, 'Oh, Richie! You are working with Richie!' I would consider The Bakery to be one of Chicago's classic restaurants, and it was unique for many reasons including the food and the atmosphere."

Gary Johnson, President, Chicago History Museum: "We knew about the famous Bakery in the sense that we used to live down the block from the restaurant on Webster Street. My wife and I were neighbors of The Bakery, and it always impressed us so much that they were out there scrubbing that sidewalk every morning. We would see Chef Louis Szathmary standing in front of his place 'cracking the whip.' Then, these buses would come from the suburbs and their riders would stream right into the restaurant. Oz Park was the neighborhood when we lived there and a lot of the signs in the Oz Park neighborhood were in Spanish. It hadn't really gentrified at that time and The Bakery was an outpost all those years. Unfortunately, while we have memories of The Bakery being a 'good neighbor,' we didn't eat there because it was too expensive for us."

Howard Altman, Chicago: "When we were first married, our favorite restaurant was a place called The Bakery. This would be in the mid- to late 60s and I remember that a full dinner at The Bakery was five bucks and that was

Two prominent restaurateurs of the 1970s who created several popular eateries were Mel Markon (Mel Markon's, Xanadu, Dixie Que, and in 2011, Bia for Mia), and George Badonsky (The Brewery, Tango, Le Bastille, George's, Maxim's de Paris). Karen and Tony Barone designed some of these restaurants; shown here is the beautiful and romantic interior of Tango, a fine seafood house located inside the Belmont Hotel from 1971 until 1986 (photo by Alexandre Georges).

The genial and effervescent Chef Louis Szathmary graced the cover of this cookbook, published by NTC/Contemporary Publishing Co. in 1975.

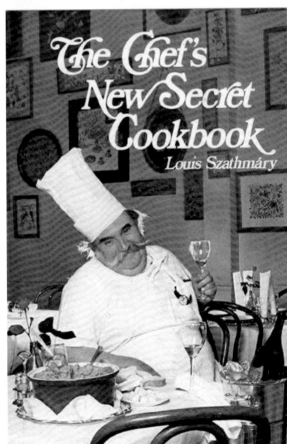

our big night out—that was our big restaurant, our go-to fine dining restaurant. There were a million other places, but The Bakery was it! Louis Szathmary owned The Bakery and now there is a small lane called Louis Szathmary Lane where the restaurant used to be."

Sheila Schlaggar: "The Bakery was a very small place and it had only one seating for dinner each night. Chef Szathmary was very temperamental and very high-strung, and if he didn't like you, he wouldn't serve you. But it was a fun place and the food was excellent."

Then, there have been a wide range of outstanding Chicago restaurants, including Le Francais, Le Perroquet, Jovan, Trio, Charlie Trotter's, Les Nomades, Chez Paul, Morton's, Eli's The Place for Steak, Trio, Gibsons, Hugo's Frog Bar and Fish House, Gordon, Gene and Georgetti, Girl & the Goat, Boka, GT Fish & Oyster, Carlos, Vie, Arun, Blackbird, Frontera Grill, and Jackie's.

Gordon Sinclair, Owner, Gordon: "When I opened my restaurant, it had a 60-person dining capacity and I ran it by the seat of my pants. When it really seemed that I was going to be able to open Gordon, I was able to raise only about $44,000. At auction, I had bought a variety of things for the restaurant. The only new thing which I had was a three-door refrigerator that was used to hold the wine and beer. However, two friends of mine, who were designers/decorators, wanted to turn the restaurant into a showpiece. I had no problem with that idea, so our place had a very high-style chic look when it opened. In that neighborhood, one could call it a 'gem in the bush.'

When people heard about the restaurant and came to eat there, one would hold the cab while another ran in to be sure it was okay, and then they would step over anyone lying on the sidewalk. You couldn't see inside the place from the outside. That began it all, and maybe because of the Gold Coast Leather Bar across the street, some of the hairdressers who worked there helped me turn it into a popular restaurant by telling their clients to visit for dinner. That began to generate business along with a mention of the restaurant in the *Chicago Tribune Sunday Magazine* (without a picture) that called the place 'a touch of New York.' Thus, Gordon all started as a result of a conversation at a dinner party. Later, as our business grew and in order to expand the size of the restaurant, I bought the adult bookstore next door.

As for the menu, at the time it opened, I only had five entrees and they came with soup or salad. I didn't have any appetizers because I didn't know how to make them. The five entrees included a fish, meat, vegetarian, pork, and chicken dish. I had only one salad dressing (a mustard vinaigrette that

previous page
Gordon opened in July 1976. "Gem in the bush" surely described this River North pioneer's location in a sleazy hotel, sandwiched between an adult bookstore and a currency exchange. The thriving restaurant soon expanded into the neighboring storefronts.

Gordon's embellished the ceramic tile lunchroom décor of the previous tenant with draperies and other chic touches.

Gordon Sinclair poses with Chef John Terczak (courtesy of Gordon Sinclair).

Gordon A. Sinclair
Announces the Opening of His Restaurant and Bar

Gordon

512 North Clark Street
Chicago, Illinois 60610
Telephone: (312) 467-9780

Lunch: 11:30 - 2:30
Dinner: 5:30 - 10:30, 12 (weekends)
Closed Sunday

The River North neighborhood was already recognized as a hotbed for some of Chicago's newest and trendiest restaurants when, by the early 1990s, restaurateurs were eyeing the Randolph and Fulton Market areas as a potential new territory for upscale eateries. This panoramic view looks west on Randolph Street from Halsted (Eric Bronsky photo).

was the house dressing), and we only had one soup. So, if you didn't want the soup, then you would get the salad. Finally, we probably had four or five desserts available for diners.

I thought that I better get a job as a waiter somewhere in order to find out more about the restaurant business. That was how naïve I was at the time. I went to Gene Sage, who was a very popular and well-known restaurateur in Chicago, and got a job with him at the Churchill Hotel, which later became a condominium across from the Ambassador East Hotel. I was 40 years old, so it probably could be classified as my midlife crisis. When I worked with Gene Sage, he had me go through ten days of training as a captain in his French restaurant called Mon Petit across the hall from his very popular place named Eugene's. I nearly wore out a tuxedo doing that training, and I also became the wine sommelier. At that time, I didn't know anything about wines, although I guess that I knew more than some of the customers. And, when the maître d' was off, I ran the restaurant on Sunday and Monday, and that did give me some experience. I was there for about six months while also working at Gordon at the time.

I would work at Gordon during the day and then go to work at the
Churchill from 4:30 p.m. until midnight. The sous-chef who was working in
the kitchen at Eugene's and Mon Petit (they used the same kitchen) wanted to
come with me, but he quit before I opened Gordon. I think that was a
precursor for things to come because he left when he was offered a chef's job
at a country club paying twice as much as I was able to pay him. I opened
Gordon with my sous-chef as my chef, but the last time I saw him, he was
chasing a waiter down the alley with a knife. My new chef walked in one day
when I was working lunch. His name was John Terczak and he worked that
night. He was really good, and his late brother, Dennis Terczak, had several
restaurants himself. John was with me for seven and a half years.

We began to broaden the menu at Gordon as John's talents developed.
We added hors d'oeuvres, the first one being artichoke fritters béarnaise, and
I had that on our menu for 25 years. Diners would come into the restaurant
because they had heard about the fritters and most ended up ordering the
artichoke fritters béarnaise.

Eventually the neighborhood began to change around Gordon. At first,
art galleries came in because they always seemed to search out places
with inexpensive rents. Al Friedman's father, who began in what is now

River North, had that whole block where Frontera Grill is located. So, a couple of galleries opened up there and then Gordon was popular on the street. In fact, it was our restaurant that Al Friedman credited with beginning the development of River North and I became known as the 'Prince of River North.' Soon, I took over the check cashing place next to the restaurant and added a lounge and a coat room since we had been using my office for a coat room at the back of the restaurant. To put it mildly, we were a 'seat of the pants' operation at the beginning.

We grew into one of the premier Chicago restaurants, but that happened later. Back then, there was only one food magazine—*Gourmet Magazine*—and there were no others since they didn't have Bon Appetit or Food and Wine at that time. There were few top restaurants in the area in the early years, including Louis Szathmary's The Bakery, and Jovan Trboyevic's place Jovan, and then the A.B. Dick corporate restaurant.

I decided to close Gordon because I was 65 years old, and I didn't want to sign another lease. I was concerned that it would tie me down for 10–15 more years, and I just thought it was time to retire. I didn't sell it because those offers included my staying there for at least another year, and I wasn't comfortable being a shill in somebody else's restaurant. I didn't need to do it, so I just closed the restaurant."

Chef Paul Kahan, Executive Chef/Owner; and Donnie Madia, Co-Owner, Blackbird, Avec, Publican, and Big Star:

Chef Paul Kahan: "I started interviewing for chef jobs through a combination of informational interviews and cooking demonstrations. I had a list of people whom I was calling every day. David Rosenthal was one of them, and he connected me with Donnie Madia. We opened Blackbird together and were fortunate that Donnie had a great friend who was the designer, Thomas Schlesser. He ended up designing Blackbird, and we immediately received accolades for the vision of the restaurant, the food, the design, and the service.

It's funny that *Chicago Magazine* gave us two stars, while everyone else raved that Blackbird was incredible because it was loud and diners sat at close quarters. Then, *Chicago Magazine* relented and gave us three stars, and later awarded us three and a half stars. I don't think that we ever want to be a four-star restaurant, because it is not what we tried to become. And while Larry Levy and Rich Melman were opening concept restaurants, our concept was great food, great service, great wine, and great design.

Chef Paul at work in Blackbird's kitchen.

The immensely popular restaurants co-owned by Chef Paul Kahan and Donnie Madia are located in the up-and-coming West Randolph and Fulton Street Market area. The Blackbird Restaurant, with its white color scheme, sparkles like a jewel.

From my standpoint, we have the perfect location because it is almost equidistant between Orchestra Hall and the United Center. And, in December 1997, it was the era in which the Bulls were starting to peak in their championship run. But we had a full cycle year of 1998, which was the last year Michael Jordan was there, and we ended up catching the end of the Jordan era. At that time, people were still hustling to go to the Bulls games and still spending a lot of money. Once the word got out that this little restaurant had intelligent food, fresh ingredients, was small, and designed like a white gypsum board box, people really started coming to eat at Blackbird. It is a perfect canvas because it is just white, and the rest is the food and the people. I think that our really unique clientele was drawn to this. People would go in there and say, wow, the food is incredible, but it is too loud and I am not coming back. There were other people who would understand it because it has really high energy and isn't like going to a gastronomic temple where you can hear a pin drop. It is a completely different experience because it is fun, and the food is equally fun and new and fresh, and we changed the menu on a regular basis.

The restaurant was packed at 7:30 p.m. on a Tuesday night in March after it had been open for 13+ years, and I don't think there are very many places that can say that. Yet the challenges that the restaurant has provided over the years have been muffled a little bit, and I know that the clientele is a little older from 20 to 60, but is a great cross section and getting younger by the year. It is the same with Avec located next door, which is an equally iconic restaurant.

At Blackbird we never tried to rush the customer out of the place, and, as time went on we made the conscious decision that Blackbird was all about quality over quantity. I think that we push that more and, honestly, I don't think that the restaurant has ever done better than it is doing now.

After Blackbird, we opened Avec, and then Publican. At Avec, we also don't push our diners out of there. People wait and they drink and they're jammed in and they love it. Our philosophy is that we want a busy operation that while you don't sit there for four hours, if you choose to stay for those four hours then you can do that, and there is little we can do about it.

Avec is in tight quarters, even tighter than Blackbird, and probably louder with incredibly high energy. We took a lot of ideas from things that we saw in New York that people were doing, including serving wine in carafinas as opposed to glasses. Eddie Seitan's wine list at Avec is incredibly affordable, and he focuses on lesser known wine regions of the world. For example, no one was really serving wine from Sardinia or any of these other crazy places where he finds his wine, including sun-drenched areas of the Mediterranean.

Avec's innovative interior design helped to popularize communal seating in Chicago.

The Publican also features a cutting-edge interior by Thomas Schlesser.

(Photo of Publican's sign by Eric Bronsky; all other photos courtesy of Restaurant Intelligence Agency).

What kind of nutty guys say that their wine lists are about sun-drenched areas of the Mediterranean Sea? And, we are doing a restaurant where everyone sits together, and if you need to get up and move, you get up and move. We are serving food in cast iron pots that come piping hot from wood-burning ovens. Really, no one had that mindset. And then you start to see restaurants with the same type of design elements popping up, and places with similar seating ideas where everyone has a table for a while. In addition, everyone seems to be using these little pots. We didn't invent any of this stuff, but we put all of these influences together and made this restaurant focus on seasonal and local products that are very simply and wonderfully prepared by our chef.

If you take it to the next step, Publican is the same kind of thing where we wanted to do a restaurant that was unique. I think that at one of our brainstorming meetings we said, let's do a place where we are revolting against the idea of gastropubs, which were a big trend at the time."

Chef Rick Bayless, Chef/Owner, Frontera Grill, Topolobampo, and XOCO: "One of the things about Frontera Grill is that it is not a concept restaurant and, like my other restaurants, expresses the kind of food about which I am very passionate. I lived for many years in central and southern Mexico and they eat food down there that most Americans wouldn't even recognize as Mexican food. Yes, there are tortillas on the table, and you may see a salsa here and there, but you probably wouldn't call it salsa. To me, Mexican food is the most complex and wondrous food in the world, and to be able to offer that in a restaurant is what I really wanted to be able to do. The true nature, and the variety and complexity of real Mexican food, is offered at my restaurants since I have developed a very solid knowledge about that food.

Topolobampo is quite different from Frontera Grill since Frontera is a very casual, boisterous, and loud place, and all the appetizers are served family-style. The entrees can also be served family-style if you request them. It is very much the kind of atmosphere you go to celebrate with a big group of people. Topolobampo is definitely four-star fine dining. It is very modern and interpretive, so we start with Mexican classics and then give them what we hope our diners understand and appreciate, which is a very modern approach to those flavors. Occasionally we deconstruct something or we re-plate it, but we spend a lot more time constructing, creating, prepping, and producing every plate of food. In fact, we have to spend over twice as much time at Topolobampo, which is almost three times as much time on each plate of food as we spend at Frontera.

Our third restaurant, XOCO, is a quick-service place where you stand in line, order your food, and then sit down because we bring it to you. It really is like the classic street food approach to Mexican cooking. When you go to a street stall in Mexico, it features a couple of different things, and only those things because they perfect just a few dishes. So, what we have in XOCO is a focus on two things: caldos, which are meal-in-a-bowl soups; and tortas, which are Mexican sandwiches that we toast in a wood-burning oven. We have varieties in each one of those categories, but you go to XOCO for a torta or a caldo. Then, you can round out your meal with some amazing hot chocolate, which we begin with cacao beans that we bring in from Mexico and grind them in a very laborious process that takes about five hours. We make our own chocolate at XOCO and then make five different kinds of hot chocolate. We serve this in classic Mexican style with churros, which are little fritters that we fry to order."

Chef Rick Bayless' award-winning showcases of fine Mexican cuisine are conjoined in three restored late 19th century buildings along a once-squalid stretch of North Clark Street. (Eric Bronsky photo).

Chef Jackie Shen, Founder and Owner, Jackie's; and currently Executive Chef, Chicago Cut Steakhouse: "When Jean Banchet, who had created Le Francais, was opening up La Mer with Arnie Morton at the Newberry, he needed a salad girl. Although I didn't know anything about making salads, I went into the kitchen and told them that I was their salad girl. Their response to me was 'Go wash that lettuce!' I looked at the lettuce and asked, 'How do I wash this lettuce?' One of the men who worked in the kitchen showed me how to do that and how to prep. Afterwards, I think that although I was just kind of thrown in there, I learned how to do the right things in the kitchen. It was a fantastic learning experience, and I also learned how to prepare fish. So when the guy quit, I wanted to have his job, but I was told that the only way I could have that position was for me to be able to prep both the salad and the fish. It meant that I would have to be at the restaurant at 7 a.m. each morning. But I was also interested in making pastries and I learned how to do that. As a result, and since it was a small kitchen, I was able to learn all the separate departments. During that time, I also worked at La Mer, and on my one day off, I would travel north to Wheeling to work at Le Francais because that was where my husband was working as a sommelier. The best thing about Jean Banchet and Le Francais was that Jean was a professional and the best way that he could express himself was to yell at his staff. So, the goal of those who worked for him was to perform so well that he wouldn't yell at us. It meant that we had to achieve his standard plus more, and that was how we learned to do the best we could while working for him.

When my husband was working at the Ritz Carlton, he found a location for us to open a new restaurant on Lincoln Avenue in Lincoln Park which was, at that time, a vegetarian restaurant during the 'hippie days' of the 1970s. I had saved up about $40,000, and with that money it helped me to open a new restaurant we called Jackie's, located at 2478 N. Lincoln Avenue, in 1982. We had a simple and inexpensive menu because we didn't know how much it would cost and we didn't want to charge too much money to our customers. One advantage that I had in 1982 was the fact that I was the first Asian woman to open up a French restaurant with French- and Asian-infused cuisine. I was the inventor of the chocolate bag and, in my first restaurant review, the Chicago Tribune gave us two and a half stars, and we stayed in business for 13 years."

Chicago Cut Steakhouse enjoys a prime location overlooking the Chicago River. It was named one of *Esquire's Best New Restaurants in America 2011* (Eric Bronsky photo).

Kevin Boehm and Rob Katz, owners, Boka Restaurant Group:

Rob: "I believe that since there are only a few of us in the restaurant business who have been able to open multiple restaurants, the key issue is to have a well-functioning infrastructure. When we first opened Boka together, Kevin and I had 40 staff, while today, there are about 500 people in our operation."

Kevin: "People make the mistake of, after having one restaurant which is very successful, taking all of their talented people from that place and moving them to new restaurants. But to us, since restaurant number one was successful and special, we are not going to hurt the first restaurant in order to make a new place better. We invest in people, chefs, and talent, and that is what you have to do to get bigger. You need to hire enough talented people, continue to support them, and provide opportunities for individual growth. We have learned that the key issue is to try to avoid any one of our employees providing bad service or food quality. If that happens, it clearly affects our reputation and the future of our business."

Rob: "People used to ask us, 'Are you going to open up another of your restaurants? It seems that you guys aren't at the restaurant that much anymore.' But, Kevin and I are very motivated and driven guys and we were not content with having just one success. I can assure you that we didn't have to talk to each other about how to operate a restaurant since it is just our nature and who we are. We can have one restaurant and it can make oodles of money, but we are still challenged by the whole process of opening a restaurant, creating the vision, putting a team together, including the architecture of the deal, and bringing something to life. It is an adrenaline rush to do that, and we are very passionate about our restaurants. I can recall nights that we'd spend at the bar together at Boka, after everyone was long gone, and it would be just the two of us sipping a glass of wine and analyzing the day's events. Then, we would go right into mapping out how we could open up a new place in 18 months, how it might be different, and whether we should offer the diners another type of cuisine."

Kevin: "Usually we have a concept in mind and then we look for a location, but, every once in a while, a great building becomes available which we think would be a wonderful spot for a restaurant. One example is the place that became GT Fish and Oyster. We loved the place where that restaurant is now located and then had to decide what would be a good restaurant for that site. We went through our list of restaurant ideas and matched a concept with that location."

Rob: "We also discuss the competition located near potential new restaurants. We both realized that we may have spent too much time opening restaurants in Lincoln Park where the deals were better. But, we also understood that there was a ceiling to what more we could do in the Lincoln Park neighborhood."

Kevin: "We actually 'sharpened our teeth' in that neighborhood and we understand that Lincoln Park is a magnificent place to live and shop. Admittedly, it has been very good to us but we literally were unaware that we had one hand tied behind our back by not expanding to other neighborhoods in the city. We had to work so hard to get to where we are, so when other neighborhoods like River North became available to us, we jumped at the opportunity."

Rob: "As for the locations of our restaurants, Boka is in Lincoln Park, Perennial is also in Lincoln Park on the edge of Old Town, Girl & the Goat is in the West Loop, and GT Fish is in River North. Sometimes we look at what has been done in a particular neighborhood before we open there. We already know that River North restaurants can make about $8–$10 million annually, on a continuous basis. When we came to the West Loop, the neighborhood was actually going through a pretty rough time. It had boomed with the KDK Group when they had Marche, Red Light and Vivo, and they helped that neighborhood grow. But, quite frankly, after so many years without new restaurants in the area, when the recession hit it seemed to be that there was a void.

Kevin and I realized that those earlier restaurants had already laid out the blueprint for the West Loop and could bring in big business as well as the fact that the Blackhawks and the Bulls were just on the doorstep of great championship runs for years and years to come."

Kevin: "In terms of opening restaurants in the city's theater district, it is a challenge because restaurants that become pre-theater staples have that as their identity, and they don't easily attract a crowd that is independent of curtain time. You have to fill up for the theater all at once and the diners all leave at the same time. It voids you of energy and then you have to build up business at the restaurant all over again. You can't flat seat the whole restaurant to get the energy back, and it dooms some of those places."

Rob: "We have been lucky with Boka because for eight years we have been able to walk that fine line by not having our business dependent on the theater crowds, while at the same time developing a loyal following. In Chicago, the entire city seems to want dinner reservations between 7:30 p.m. and 8:00 p.m., while in New York it is different because people dine until 11 or 11:30 p.m. each night."

Kevin: "As for the creation of Girl & the Goat, there is an interesting story of how Chef Stephanie Izard got involved with us. It was a combination of both her coming to us and us approaching her. Stephanie was having dinner one night at Boka when Rob and I were there. We both walked up to her table to say hello since we had known her during her days at Scylla. She was taping *Top Chef* at the time and we said to her, 'When you are done with your dinner, we are going to be down at Landmark, so why don't you walk over there and say hello.' That night she came to Landmark and we all had a drink together. Of course, she couldn't tell us how she was doing on *Top Chef, but she looked really happy. The only thing she knew at the time was* that she had made it to the finals of the show. In fact, she couldn't even tell us that information because she was under contract with the show, and

Stephanie is a woman of her word. So, we just said to her, 'When you are done with the show, give us a call sometime.'"

Rob: "Lo and behold, she was selected as the winner of *Top Chef* that year, and then our phone rang. It was a big deal when she won although I don't think that Kevin and I ever thought again about our previous conversation. Her victory was good for her and provided some great opportunities. When she called and set up the meeting with us at Perennial, Stephanie had a very clear vision of what she wanted to do with a new restaurant. At the time, her views of the future were closely in line with what Kevin and I thought was very sensible for a restaurant concept, and we just said to her that we loved her dining ideas and thought that we would be very fortunate to do something with her. She is one of the few people who actually came to us with a restaurant concept and wanted to lever our infrastructure with her ability to cook her own food. When Stephanie worked at Scylla, she had to combine the roles of being general manager, maître d', kitchen manager, and chef. It was a very small restaurant and it was overwhelming. She gave it such a great go and it was a beloved restaurant, but I think that she said, 'Enough of that. I want to focus on what I am doing, and maybe the Boka boys can help with the infrastructure and the partnership by doing it that way.'"

Kevin: "Originally, she was looking at opening a restaurant in Logan Square in a much smaller location. Rob and I said to her, 'We think that you will be very busy with your new restaurant, so you need to be located where you can attract a lot of diners.' In our minds, we were thinking of a restaurant that was twice the size of what she had in mind. And, we thought that way because even with the size that we have right now, Rob and I have never seen anything like this before. It not only takes three months to get a reservation at Girl & the Goat, but every time slot on every single day is filled."

Rob: "Nothing lasts forever, but it is past the honeymoon stage for her place and it has been open more than a year already. Word of mouth has helped build her business, and it is not only because she is famous from television. She is beloved for many reasons, and the restaurant speaks to a lot of different people. So, for us and for her, there was pressure because this was her shot to make it a very successful restaurant. Now, because we were involved too, it has to be perfect. In addition, we opened it during the worst economic times of the past 75 years, so it required us to make all the right decisions and to have impeccable timing. It probably didn't develop as fast as we all wanted, especially for her, yet despite our impatience, she was quite brilliant

Since its inception in 2003, Boka Restaurant Group has emerged as one of the most successful chef-driven restaurant groups in the country.

In 2011, BRG owned five restaurants including Boka and Girl & The Goat (Eric Bronsky photos).

with her ability to combine use of social media, marketing, and creating these underground, creative goat dinners to build the business. As Kevin said, we almost signed a deal to open it on Milwaukee Avenue near Division Street, and quite frankly, we are lucky that we didn't. We always were pushing for a more high profile neighborhood, although the West Loop represented a compromise since it is very busy and close enough to the Loop and the sporting events. It has turned out to be a great business move."

One of the LEYE restaurants that is truly a Chicago classic has been Everest with Chef John Joho as the chef/owner since it opened in 1987.

Chef Jean Joho, Chef/Partner, Everest: "I came to Chicago in 1984 to reopen Maxim's de Paris here with George Badonsky and five assistant chefs. In terms of fine dining, this was a big push and the restaurant had a huge impact on the city. Fine dining was always available in Chicago, but I wanted to bring an updated version of fine dining like what was happening in France. I was shocked that some people called restaurants fine dining when they served onion soup and escargots because in France that would be considered more as a country-style restaurant. Ours was the first restaurant in 1984 where diners could walk in and be treated to a tasting menu.

There is no disputing Everest's position among Chicago's foremost classic restaurants of all time. Chef Jean Joho has presided over the Everest kitchen since 1987 (photo courtesy of Lettuce Entertain You Enterprises).

Everest's dining room (photo courtesy of Lettuce Entertain You Enterprises).

We also had two cheese carts and a cheese sommelier, so it meant that Maxim's was a big revolution in Chicago dining at that time. They were also one of the first to offer petit fours and chocolate at the end of the meal.

While I was a French-born chef, I also spent many years in Italy. I had the first restaurant in Chicago, and maybe in the United States, to have a la minute risotto made from 100 percent organic carnaroli rice, and I remember that the *New York Times* did an article about me, reporting that I served the best risotto in the United States. But, being in Italy, France, and Germany, it was very easy for me to make Italian food because I spoke those languages and knew the European-style presentation of food.

In 1987, I partnered with Richard Melman and Lettuce Entertain You Enterprises to open Everest. In the same way as I developed Maxim's, my focus had been to have a fine dining restaurant. At Everest, I wanted the menu selections to represent the Alsace region in France of my childhood, so I created many connections with Alsace wineries and soon established the most extensive wine list in the world from those vineyards.

For the first couple of years, Everest was confusing to people because it was a private club for lunch and then a restaurant that was open to the public for dinner. We converted the club to a full-time public restaurant in 1986. From the beginning, I only used fresh American ingredients, which were very limited at the time. Since you have every type of food in this country, my feeling was to use a wide range of offerings and find people from whom we could buy those foods, even though, in 1986, it was really difficult to use only American products. The true meaning of the term 'fine French dining' was often misinterpreted because it was not readily available at that time. Often, they called it intercontinental cuisine, which was the food from nowhere or anywhere.

From the beginning, dinner time was very successful, and since then, 25 years later, we are still open and a popular restaurant. My philosophy has always been that what is good enough for me today is not good enough tomorrow, and I am always trying to improve what I am doing because the day that you stop improving is when you fail, and just maintaining things is not going to work.

At Everest, I wanted to be able to make great European-style bread but was unable to achieve the quality I was looking for due to the restrictions on the facilities. So, I once again partnered with Rich Melman and Lettuce Entertain You Enterprises to create Corner Bakery. While I have always liked American-style sandwiches, I missed the type of bread available in Europe. When Corner Bakery became a big success, Brinker International bought out the company from Lettuce Entertain You. Many times in business you have to make such decisions, and in the case of Corner Bakery, it was a good one.

Next, I opened Brasserie Jo in the mid-1990s on Hubbard Street, and it became another of our very successful restaurants. At the time we opened, it was the only French brasserie in Chicago, and it was new, casual, fun food, inexpensive, and a place where you could go five or six nights a week. It had a good atmosphere and very mixed clientele with all level of incomes and demographics. When we closed Brasserie Jo, we tried to decide what to have for our next restaurant. We knew that we couldn't be sentimental about it and should just think about what would be happening for the next 20 years. So, what I have done now with Rich, Jerrod, and RJ is to create a brand new concept at Paris Club that replaced Brasserie Jo.

We opened a Brasserie Jo in Boston, and then Eiffel Tower in Las Vegas. Eiffel Tower offers updated French classic food and is the premier French restaurant in Las Vegas. I am very proud that I was able to offer the restaurant's recipes in a special cookbook published just last year.

I feel that when I can help the younger generation, I like to do that, and since Rich and I work very well together and have mutual respect for each other, we have been able to create several new restaurants. Rich's strengths and mine clearly complement each other. Together we combine my culinary style with his creative vision and leadership. I think that Rich and I have had a very dynamic collaboration that has allowed us to be successful together and as a company.

Looking back, Chicago has had many classic restaurants over the years, including such places as The Bakery and Jovan's Le Perroquet. Jovan was an icon, but he served what he wanted to serve and he told the diner what he wanted them to eat. Is he a classic? At the time, he was classic, but I don't know if that would be the case today. I am sure that

The Pump Room, during its height, was a classic, but it is there in name only. I think that what happened to The Pump Room is more than the fact that the stars didn't go there anymore. There is nothing wrong with the room, but it was a new generation who no longer had a strong interest in eating prime rib, Yorkshire pudding and flaming bananas. So, you have to keep up to date in order to survive and flourish in the restaurant business.

Over my years in Chicago, I have seen a great evolution of all cuisine in the city. We now have educated diners who are demanding a higher level of food and service. All fine restaurants today are fulfilling such expectations by their customers, and I feel great pride in being a leader in that growth. I plan to continue to learn and grow and keep bringing the best quality products and dining experience to our guests."

In 1973, Chef Jean Banchet opened Le Francais, a restaurant that would become one of the highest rated French restaurants in America, and Banchet made the decision to locate it in Chicago's northwest suburb of Wheeling. Not only was the food and service outstanding, but it became a training ground for several sous and pastry chefs who would become famous after their years working under Banchet. The restaurant's appetizers, entrees, and desserts amazed dinner guests, or at least those who could even secure a reservation and afford the steep prices to dine there.

Kevin J. Brown: "In 1979, Gabino and I met at Le Francais in Wheeling and the owner/chef of the restaurant, Jean Banchet knew Gabino was going to eat there. It was clear that Banchet, wanted to demonstrate to Gabino what he had at the restaurant, and it was like, 'Okay, just watch what I can do and you're not going to steal any of my thunder.' It turned out to be one of the most magnificent meals I ever ate. In fact, early on in the meal they brought out Pheasant consommé that had the en croute on top. What happens is that they put it underneath you and they have a little cutout where the dough is located, and it is closed so it pops naturally. I had never experienced food like that in my whole life, and the courses just kept on coming. About halfway through...and we were drinking a lot of wine...my head was spinning. I remember Banchet saying to me, 'What year were you born?' My answer was 1955, and the next thing I knew they were serving a '55 Margeaux, and this wasn't the same type of wine I may have taken to The Bakery. It was a spectacular bottle of wine, something I had never had in my life. I think that Le Francais was the Alinea of its time, and that night I decided I wanted to be in dining as my career. Also knowing that Ambria was going to open soon, it stoked my passion for food and my vision of what

Jovan Trboyevic presided over Le Perroquet with authority and meticulous attention to detail. In the background is Chef Gabino Sotelino, who would later partner with Rich Melman (Eric Bronsky Collection).

entertainment and dining could be. In fact, I believe that Ambria provided Chicago with the certain sophistication and style that one only found in New York City.

Betty Schaffel: "I got to go to Le Francais once because my son, who is a physician, was invited there for a dinner being hosted by a pharmaceutical company. Everything they served was creamy and rich and made with butter and oh, so delicious. What impressed me about the place was their use of different fish forks and fish knives. If you were having meat, you would have a different knife and fork than if you were having fish. If you were having salad, you would have a cold plate and the desserts... well, it was just a fabulous dinner. Everything about the meal was elegant, but what struck me as odd was that the pharmaceutical company was doing a presentation about a new drug for treating high cholesterol and heart disease!"

Bob Darling: "We had a group of six that regularly traveled, did fine dining, and theater together. One evening, we went up to Le Francais for dinner and one of the guys in our party wanted his steak well done and they refused to prepare it that way. He was livid and caused quite a scene. The five of us were kind of squirming and shifting our eyes up towards the ceiling, then down towards the floor. I think he wound up having to order something else and proceeded to sulk all night. It put a damper on what was quite an expensive experience and what should have been a very special night."

Dan O'Day: "The first time I ever went to Le Francais, I was on an expense account and took a client there. I sold advertising space for the *Chicago Sun-Times*. They had two seatings for dinner. I was with my boss, and we took a local grocery chain owner who advertised rather heavily in our paper to dinner there. We really wanted to take him someplace special, and I wanted to see what it was like, too. There were six of us, the client, my boss and me, plus our wives. While waiting for the place to be cleared from the first seating, the diners were exiting and who came walking out? None other than Marshall Field V, who owned the *Chicago Sun-Times*. I knew him a little bit—after all, I'd been working there some 25 years. He saw me and said, 'Dan O'Day—so this is where you spend my money entertaining clients.' I responded with 'Mr. Field, I'd like you to meet (client's name). He places about 60 percent of his advertising budget in our paper.' Mr. Field said, 'It's a pleasure to meet you and I hope you enjoy your dinner. I'm glad to see that Dan is spending our money on a good client like you.' In all honesty, the irony of it was Marshall Field V probably didn't know how much we spend entertaining clients, but it was funny to run into him at such a fine restaurant as Le Francais."

Susan Herman: "The first time I ever had escargot was at Le Francais, and I was having a struggle with it. The snail, buried in a pound and a half of butter and garlic, absolutely refused to come out of the shell. I kept going after it with the little fork and it started to come out, but then it zipped back in. I did everything I could think of short of pounding it on the table. So, I finally got hold of the waiter and said, 'Excuse me, but the snail will not come out of the shell.' And he said, 'Well, suck it.' I said, 'Excuse me?' He said, 'Just suck on it and it will come out.' And he was right. Other than having startled me with his comment, that was how I had my first escargot."was known for its nouvelle cuisine. It set a standard for its seafood and meat dishes, and Jovan is considered to be one of the greatest chefs in the history Chicago's classic restaurants. Chef Jovan also operated Jovan restaurant, as well as the private club called Les Nomades, which opened in 1978. After he retired, the restaurant was sold to Mary Beth Liccioni of Le Francais fame."

Janet Davies, ABC 7 Chicago, Host and Executive Producer, 190 North: "After living in this area for several years, we moved to the southern part of the United States and I was gone from the Midwest for quite some time. However, my next memory of eating at a Chicago restaurant happened in 1978–1979 when I was working in Cincinnati, Ohio and came to Chicago on a press junket to see two movies. One was *The China Syndrome,* and the other was the Gregory Peck movie about Damien. When the junket was over, and this meant that the stars would be traveling the country being interviewed about their movies, the particular publicist in charge of the junket took all of us out for dinner. Lucky for me because we were taken to the classic restaurant, Le Perroquet, located on Walton just off of Michigan Avenue. At that restaurant you had to walk upstairs to the dining room. It was the first time I had ever experienced fine French food, and they served a Grand Marnier soufflé that was unbelievable. The place was dimly lit and reeked of classy atmosphere, the food was unbelievable, and I didn't have to pay for it since I was with all these other young journalists. I was just a 'small town girl' at that point, even though Cincinnati wasn't a small town. I do recall the owner of Le Perrroquet, the famous Jovan Trboyevic, and the fact that we were warned to be on our best behavior because he would not entertain us and would probably kick us out of the restaurant if we misbehaved. We were told not to be loud, rude, or drink too much. Later on, Jovan also opened another of my favorite restaurants, Les Nomades, and, once again, he insisted that people who came to his restaurants to dine needed to act like ladies and gentlemen. I would argue that his places, including Le Perroquet, Jovan, and Les Nomades, were all classic Chicago restaurants."

Bob Darling: "Les Nomades is still in existence and reviewed every month in *Chicago Magazine*. The food and service were always fantastic. Years ago, some friends invited me as their guest to the Law Review—the show the lawyers put on every year. I wanted to reciprocate, so I said to my friend Joanne Will of the *Chicago Tribune* that I would like to take them to Les Nomades. Joanne was a member and she said we could use her membership. She told me that they only take cash, so I asked her how much she thought it was going to be per person. She gave me a figure and I padded it a bit, just to be on the safe side. When we sat down and started to eat, I began to mentally add up what the meal was going to cost and I had nowhere near the money to pay for this dinner. Now what? I can hardly eat, I can hardly swallow. Suddenly, inspiration hit. About a month after this dinner, Joanne and another friend and I were going to Europe, including Yugoslavia. Jovan, the owner of Les Nomades, was from Yugoslavia. So, I excused myself from the table and I went to find him and explain the situation. I told him I could give him what I had with me and that I would leave my watch and come back the next day with the balance. I told him I was there with Ms. Will and I didn't want to be embarrassed or cause a scene. He was so kind and gracious and said it was no problem. Then he asked if I would like to become a member. Well, I thought he was the coolest guy on two feet, and when I returned

The success of Gibsons, open since
1989, led to the launch of
Hugo's Frog Bar, specializing in seafood,
and Luxbar, a neighborhood saloon
(Eric Bronsky photos).

to our table, I said that I had just gone up to Jovan to seek a little information about Yugoslavia for our upcoming trip. After that experience, I took some friends there annually for dinner because to me, Les Nomades was in a class all by itself."

There are many great steakhouses in Chicago including Gene and Georgetti, Chicago Chop House, and Chicago Cut Steakhouse, among others. Probably the most popular, in terms of customer volume and revenue, has been Gibsons. This restaurant is located on Rush Street next to another very popular restaurant, Hugo's Frog Bar and Fish House, with both dining establishments owned by Steve Lombardo and Hugo Ralli, the principals of Gibsons Restaurant Group.

Steve Lombardo: "The location of Gibsons was previously a drugstore, and then the famous Mister Kelly's, before it became the site of our current restaurant. The original building burned down in the 1960s and was rebuilt as Mister Kelly's, which remained open until 1974. The rebuilt version included additional seats because it had become too small for a popular entertainment venue. In addition to Barbra Streisand performing there, the entertainers included Bette Midler, Barry Manilow, and a wide variety of comedians that included Mort Sahl, Shelley Berman, and Bob Newhart. Jazz stars performed primarily the London House, another Marienthal Brothers place, located at Michigan and Wacker, and they also could be seen at The Happy Medium on Rush Street, as well as at Mister Kelly's. Barbra Streisand was an unknown when she first sang at Mister Kelly's, and after she made it big time, she performed here for $5,000 a week even after recording her very successful album, *Color Me Barbra.* She liked the Marienthals and although she could have bought out her contract with them, she decided to continue performing at Mister Kelly's.

Rush Street was a hot street when Mister Kelly's, the Gate of Horn, and The Happy Medium were open. In addition, there were so many nightclubs here with some big star performing almost every night. Today, there are approximately 15–20 restaurant/bars located on Rush Street between Ontario and Division, but there was a time when there were 150 of those places.

I used to be an owner in a restaurant called Hot Spurs and a bar/nightclub called PVC on Division Street. One day, I was walking down the street with one of my buddies who informed me that the Marienthals had sold this site (formerly Mister Kelly's) to some of their staff. Then, coincidentally, one of the Marienthal's sons had just gotten his driver's license and had rear ended my buddy's car when he was getting off the expressway. It wasn't a bad accident and only involved $400-$500 damage, but the kid said to my buddy, 'It was my fault, and if you don't call the police, I will pay for it.

My dad owns Mister Kelly's and I'll have him call you.' So, they exchanged information, and his father called him and said that whatever the damages were he would pay for them. The guy said that he had a restaurant on Division near Mister Kelly's and to just walk over and he would give him the money. About two months later we were walking down the street, and although Mister Kelly's was closed during the day, we decided to just stop in and see if he was there. We knocked on the door and started talking to Marienthal, and we ended up buying the place. In 1974, we had opened a bar called Sweetwater's, but it wasn't until 1989 when we actually opened Gibsons.

We first sold Sweetwater in 1981 but ended up having to take it back in 1986 or 1987. Those were down years for Rush Street at that time, and since I was kind of struggling along, I was also trying to figure out what to do with the place. Mayor Daley was running for election at the time, and I thought that things could change for us if he was elected. Hugo and I had partnered in the interim and we came up with a new concept for the place, and we raised some money for the venture. We opened Gibsons in May 1989, Daley took office on May 16, 1989, and things just changed positively for us.

Mayor Richard M. Daley started putting up trees around us, got the out-door cafes going, and things just got better around here. Also, the revival of North Michigan Avenue helped drive new business to us, and one can say that all the changes happening across Chicago were positive for us. Prior to that time, the River North neighborhood seemed to be dominated by flophouses, bums, and prostitutes, and things were really bad there. When the mayor cleaned up the area, built Millennium Park, and introduced all of the festivals at night during the summer, it all spilled over into our area. Plus, the new McCormick Place attracted conventioneers who also frequented our restaurants. We had plenty of new business, but the key was turning them into return customers. We became a steakhouse partly because Rich Melman was helping me with the idea, and partly because we were aiming our business in that direction. Since I am not a big fan of French food, Hugo and I talked about the focus of our restaurant and decided to have Gibsons be a great steakhouse."

Hugo Ralli: "The other reason for us being a steakhouse is that there were only about five other top steakhouses in town at that time. Now there are about 30-40 of them in Chicago, but I think that the only top ones open when we began included Gene and Georgetti, Chicago Chop House, the Palm, Morton's and Eli's The Place for Steak. I think that today we have become Chicago's number one steakhouse. And, per square foot, we are among the most financially successful restaurants in the country with 8,400 square feet and a worth of over $20 million. Not only are we busy here, but between our two downtown restaurants, Gibsons and Hugo's Frog Bar, and Gibsons in Rosemont, we do $35 million in annual revenues. And, although our place in Oak Brook is moving in the same direction, we are not planning to have a national chain of Gibsons restaurants."

Another of Chicago's more popular steakhouses over more than 20 years has been Harry Caray's Italian Steakhouse, which is located in the River North neighborhood.

Grant DePorter, President and Managing Partner, Harry Caray's Restaurants Group: "In 1987, Harry opened Harry Caray's Italian Steakhouse. It was going to be called H. I. Cobb because Henry Ives Cobb had been the architect of the original building. Cobb had worked on the 1893 Columbian Exposition, as well as the original Chicago Historical Society and the Potter Palmer ' castle.' Some of the partners in the restaurant didn't know who Cobb was and were close friends of Harry Caray. One of them threw out the idea that we should call the restaurant 'Harry Caray's,' and that is what we decided to do. Today, our structure is an historic landmark building and is recognized as one of the best examples of Dutch Renaissance architecture in the Midwest.

Harry led the perfect life of a restaurateur because he was either focused on baseball or being in restaurants or bars. That was his whole life, and we calculated that he drank about 300,000 alcoholic drinks in his lifetime. Maybe he didn't finish all the glasses, but he loved being with people in a restaurant and bar atmosphere. So, his seat in the bar was the one closest to the front door because he wanted to be accessible to everybody. Similarly, his seat in the dining room was the one closest to the front door. He even made sure that his home phone number was listed at 411 so that if any fan wanted to call him, they could easily get in touch. Harry would sign autographs forever, never charging for them, and he was simply the ultimate Cub fan and Bud man. He had a full life with a lot of history, including the fact that he worked for 53 years as a Major League baseball announcer, including 16 years as an announcer for the Cubs on WGN radio and television. He could really 'work a room.' He loved talking to everybody.

His wife, Dutchie Caray, really handled all the food in the Caray family, which allowed Harry to focus on what he liked to do. She is still involved in the restaurant as a partner and just loves the restaurant life, just like Harry. Dutchie has so much energy that if we ever needed her at the restaurant at 4 a.m., she would be here. I consider her a "superwoman" and someone who keeps alive the memory and spirit of Harry in Chicago and throughout the sports world today."

The flagship Harry Caray's restaurant is housed in an architectural landmark just north of Marina City and the Chicago River (Eric Bronsky photo).

Sportscaster legends Harry Caray and Jack Brickhouse (courtesy of Lettuce Entertain You Enterprises).

Charlie Trotter has been a world-renowned chef and has operated Charlie Trotter's since 1987. It is clearly one of Chicago's classic restaurants and serves a wide variety of salads, seafood, and pastas, along with a series of exquisite desserts. The restaurant is located in an old brownstone on West Armitage in the Lincoln Park neighborhood and ranks right at the top of many lists of fine dining establishments in the city. Trotter also trained many of the current and up-and-coming chefs in Chicago.

Gordon Sinclair: "Interestingly, I gave Charlie Trotter his first restaurant job, which was at Sinclair's American Grill in Lake Forest. I had done a few restaurants with Marshall Field V, including one down in Florida. I hired Charlie at the same time I had Norman Van Aken in the kitchen as a chef whom I had found in Key West, Florida. Van Aken has now become an author and a television personality. I hired Charlie when he was only 21 years old, and I thought that he was very good, very precise, and with lots of energy. We brought him into the kitchen at Marché and sent him down to Florida where he was part of the opening crew along with Van Aken to open Sinclair's American Grill in the Jupiter Beach Hilton (now it is called the Jupiter Beach Hotel)."

Some of the best known and most popular Italian restaurants in Chicago over the years have been located in Little Italy on the Near West Side. Chef Scott Harris has built a dining empire based on his success at the various Francesca restaurants.

Chef Scott Harris, Founder and Executive Chef, Francesca's Restaurants: "Mia Francesca was the first restaurant that I opened with my wife, Francesca, on February 13, 1992, at 311 N. Clark Street, a couple blocks north of Belmont. We opened it with no money in the bank so it took us a couple of years to save up enough to expand our business. Our second location was in Naperville, and was called La Sorella di Francesca. Shortly after that, we opened, simultaneously, Francesca's North in Northbrook and Francesca's Little Italy on Taylor Street in 1995. We just grew from there, and I have been able to keep up with all this growth because we have great people working for our restaurants. We now have 1,700 employees and are growing rapidly and have plans to go out of state and open 100 new restaurants over the next 10 years, including two places in Arizona that are under construction. We also have three new restaurants opening in San Diego. Obviously, things have gone great for me.

Prior to opening on Taylor Street, Joe Doppes, who owns Taylor Street Bistro as well as Chez Margot on Wall Street, called me out of the blue and

Charlie Trotter's blends quietly into Chicago's Lincoln Park neighborhood (Eric Bronsky photo).

Francesca's Restaurants have expanded throughout the Chicago area and beyond. The restaurant shown here was the original; it opened in the Lakeview neighborhood in 1992.

Davanti Enoteca (which means literally, 'in front of wine bar') was an instant hit upon opening in Chicago's Little Italy neighborhood in 2010 (both photos courtesy of Scott Harris).

said, 'Hey, I've been to Little Italy, and I think that your restaurant will go great here.' Back then, the neighborhood was very rough, and I said to him, 'No!' In fact, the second night that we were open, we were robbed at gunpoint. He finally talked me into it, and now it is my second or third best restaurant.

I have seen the neighborhood change completely, and my goal is to really bring back Little Italy and take the old Gennaro's (owned and operated by my partner, Chef Mary Jo Gennaro) and make that into what we will call the Ball Room, which will be a meatball shop. We are also planning to own that building. I also want to have a great bakery on Taylor Street, along with one of those stores that sells knickknacks, and a couple of places that will sell gelato and bambolini (stuffed donuts with cream). In addition, I would love to open a Sicilian seafood house with seafood from the Mediterranean, and we are working on a porketta in which they take the whole pig, bone it all out, stuff it with all kinds of fun stuff, and roll it and slice it into a sandwich. So, I want to bring Little Italy back to its earlier greatness.

I really want to own every restaurant in this area because it is a great neighborhood and a great street with the hospitals and the university located here. When people come to Chicago, they know about Greektown, but I want the city to put up a sign that says 'Welcome To Little Italy.' In order to accomplish that goal, we will try to raise money from individuals who agree with my goal for Little Italy and who visit Chicago from all over the country and the world. Simply put, I want those people to seek out our Little Italy. Although there used to be some great restaurants on this street, sadly, all of the 'mom and pop' places have closed.

I consider our restaurants as classic Chicago restaurants because we serve big portions and Chicagoans are big people and big eaters. Everyone relates to our restaurants because they are reasonably priced, and I think that we are going to be here for 50 years."

One of Chef Harris' partners is Chef Mary Jo Gennaro.

Chef Mary Jo Gennaro, Chef/Owner, Salatino's: "If you look across the street from Davanti Enoteca today, you can see a bar there. That was my dad's tavern in the 1940s and early 1950s. In order to attract more customers in those days, my mother would cook a large buffet of food, and as long as men came in and spent money at the bar, they could eat the food for free. She did this every weekend, and every Saturday she would put out different types of dishes. And the men who used to drink in the bar would bring their wives and children on the weekends and everybody would eat for free. This went on for a while until, finally, my mother said to my father, 'You know, John, if I can give it away then I can sell it.' From that point on, they moved from that location two doors east and opened Gennaro's. They started out with a bar and four booths, and every day she would add some new food…home-made ravioli, prosciutto, sandwiches, and pizzas. Everybody loved our pizza.

People started coming in for dinner and that led to serving fewer pizzas. Since we only had 50 seats, my parents had to make a choice about what they were going to do: continue to serve the pizzas or the dinners. The dinners included veal parmesan, pork chops and peppers, braciola, home-made pastas, veal dishes, and chicken.

I opened Salatino's on December 28, 2010, while Gennaro's had been in business from November 1959 until December 2009. The restaurants were at different locations, with Salatino's at 626 Racine and Gennaro's at 1352 W. Taylor. I think that what distinguishes those two restaurants from other Italian restaurants has been that we serve more central Italian food. We are from Abruzzi, Italy, located about 80 miles north of Rome, and my mother was from Calabria, which is south of Rome. So, while our cooking is more southern than it is northern Italian, my mother favored the southern Italian cooking. I think that the only thing that distinguishes Salatino's from Gennaro's is location, but, other than that, they are and were the same.

I think that what made and now makes our restaurants special have been our customers. When they used to come into Gennaro's, they came specifically for the red gravy, the homemade gnocchi and ravioli, and the egg noodles. Some of the entrees that we still make today are pretty much the same as what we offered when we were on Taylor Street. People are appreciative and they love it, and they demonstrate that fact by always returning to the restaurant and eating the foods that we serve. We are a casual family restaurant, and I have had people say to me that it is a very homey atmosphere at Salatino's, and they feel like they are in an Italian mother's living room. Customers who would come to Gennaro's would say to us, 'I feel like I am eating out of an Italian mother's kitchen.' And, basically, they were. Nothing was precooked because everything was cooked to order, and my mother, Eleanor Gennaro, cooked in her restaurant just the way she cooked at home.

I think that the neighborhood Italian restaurants in Chicago are all different and all good. We are not a high-end restaurant, but I would say that we are in the middle. As far as people liking or loving particular restaurants, that's okay. We're here to support each other. Yes, we are competitors, but we all cook a little differently and everybody has their own likes and dislikes, so I don't see that as a problem. I would say that Gennaro's and Salatino's could be considered as classic restaurants from that section of the Italian community."

Salatino's, opened in late 2010, aims
to be a classic neighborhood Italian
restaurant patterned after its predecessor
Gennaro's (courtesy of Scott Harris).

Currrently the top rated restaurant in Chicago, and considered one of the best in the country, is Alinea with Chef Grant Achatz as the chef/owner. He has also recently opened up another premier restaurant called Next.

Chef Grant Achatz, Chef/Owner, Alinea and Next: "I returned to America (from Europe) reenergized and just believing in food and cooking once again. My next cooking adventure was a job as a chef at The French Laundry in Napa, California, where I was given the wonderful opportunity to work for Thomas Keller for four and a half years. Simply put, he was an amazing person who would serve as one of the key mentors in my cooking career. I then returned to the Chicago area, and I went to work at Trio in Evanston for three years. Trio, which was owned by Henry Adaniya, was awesome. I look back and realize that I have been so lucky in my life because, at various critical moments throughout my introductory years, I have had people come into my life and serve as my mentors. When I was at the French Laundry, I was 25 years old and a young kid. But I was ready to go do my own thing. I did a nationwide search of restaurateurs who were willing to let a young chef who had a very clear vision of what he wanted to accomplish with the food to come in to their restaurant and display his cooking arts, carte blanche. When you think about it, it was probably a crazy idea. Profit margins are slim with 5-15 percent of new restaurants opening and closing quickly, so if you have 'skin' in the game, you don't want to give it up.

Amazingly, I discovered that Henry Adaniya was willing to take a chance with me. He said, 'Even though you are 25 years old, have this crazy idea about food and it is a major, major risk for me, I am willing to let you do your thing in my restaurant.' My idea about food, even then, is what we do today at Alinea. I call my food style 'progressive American.' But, here we are in 2011, and progressive cuisine is not something that shocks people because it has become pretty normal over the last 10 years. Back in 2001, especially in Chicago, people didn't know how to deal with it, so it was a big risk for Henry. So we came in and opened up Trio in July 2001. In fact, we reopened it since it had been open since 1994 with Rick Tramonto and Gale Gand. We revamped the whole thing, but Henry, Rick, and Gale were all partners (that is why it was called Trio). Rick and Gale left Trio in order to open Tru in the city, and Henry held on to the restaurant. Henry hired Shawn McClain, who was the owner of Spring, Green Zebra, and Custom House in Chicago (Shawn has sold those restaurants and since moved to Las Vegas). Then, Henry took a leap of faith and hired me. I said to him that we were not doing a la carte or Asian food anymore. Instead, we were going to go really progressive, blow it off the charts, and do all this crazy stuff.

Some of the most highly acclaimed restaurants in the country specializing in progressive cuisine are located in Chicago, but their exterior facades seldom hint at the remarkable level of culinary innovation taking place within.

Alinea blends in with its surroundings on a residential street in Lincoln Park with nary a sign.

No casual observer would imagine that this 'plain Jane' building in the heart of the Fulton Street Market area is a hotbed of molecular gastronomy and postmodern cuisine. Homaro Cantu's Moto and iNG Restaurants, and Grant Achatz's Next and The Aviary, are among the building's tenants (Eric Bronsky photos).

We did exactly that and opened in 2001, but sadly, on September 11, 2001, four months later, the economy went straight down as a result of the terrorist attacks on the Twin Towers in NYC.

So, here we were, trying to do something that was new and different. As a result of 9/11, restaurant customers were gravitating towards comfort food. They wanted meat loaf and mashed potatoes and things that made them feel comfortable because everything else in the world was going crazy. Yet, we decided to offer the opposite. We said that we weren't going to go to a blue plate special, or lower our prices because the economy was sinking, or tone down our concept of food. In fact, we decided to do the opposite because we believed that Americans at that moment really wanted to forget what was going on in the world. So, instead of catering to the 'homey' side of cooking, we said that we were going to create an adventure. Just like when you go in and you watch a great movie. You sit down in a movie theater, watch the screen, and for two hours, you don't think of anything but what is on the screen. That's what we did. And, Penny Pollack said, 'This is awesome and what you guys are doing is great.' That was also the response from Phil Vettel and all of the critics said, this is something real, exciting and it is breathing life into the restaurant community here in Chicago. We kept going even though we struggled. At the very end, we were doing very well, and as a result, I had the opportunity with Nick Kokonas to open Alinea.

Alinea stands out as a dining experience, but I don't believe that it is any more special than Charlie Trotter's was in 1989 or Everest in 1987. We are breaking through now even though we opened six years ago, and I would argue that what we have done really well is to be very hands-on. I spend about 80 hours a week at the restaurant, and our general manager is there probably even more than me. I guess the only thing that we can't really quantify is our passion for the place. We have 70 employees at Alinea, and we will have over 80 employees by next year. So, what we figured out is that if people drink our 'Kool-Aid,' they are in for the dining job of their life because they love it and understand the passion and the required commitment to our style of dining. On the other hand, that same 'Kool-Aid' has scared some people away from working at our restaurant because they don't want to work that hard. They are looking for a job, not a life. What we are trying to create is a lifestyle. It is not even about punching in and out on the clock. It is about living your life and being part of a philosophy.

As for repeat customers, Alinea is a pretty pricey restaurant, but to us, a regular is someone who comes once a month. We have people who have dined at the restaurant 50-60 times and they visit us from all over the world. Twenty-five percent of our customers at Alinea are from the state of Illinois, while 75 percent are from all over the globe. Right now, I don't think that we compare with any other restaurant in Chicago on a variety of measures.

I still go back to what Charlie Trotter has done with his restaurant because I think that he put Chicago on the gastronomy map and, clearly, he also has customers who fly here from all over the world. I think that television cooking shows generally have helped all of us in the restaurant business. If you are Rick Bayless or Graham Elliot Bowles, both of whom have been on *Top Chef* and *Top Chef Masters*, their restaurants are packed because they are penetrating the interest of the general public. They are not chefs anymore…they are celebrities and they are in the mainstream.

As for opening Next and any planned restaurant expansion, I think that there are two things which are really important when you talk about growth in the number of restaurants you own and operate. I was really hesitant to expand, and not absolutely sure if I wanted to do it. Dave Beran is my head chef at Next, and if you think about working 80 hours a week for five years, that level of dedication is amazing. As a result, I thought about how to reward them. I have been very lucky and have had some wonderful opportunities. So, if I can afford to give some of those opportunities to them, I should. We opened Next so that Dave could run it. The same applies to Joe Catterson, who was the wine director at Trio in 2001. He is currently our director of operations and has been with us for 10 years. At that point you feel like expansion and subsequently, creating opportunities for people, is a good thing.

For me, I love Alinea, I love the creativity, I love going in there. We are open five nights a week, but I am there four of those nights, while usually, I am at Next on one night. It is very hard for me to create a restaurant empire because everything that we have built Alinea on has a hands-on approach. We are not doing comfort food, so it is more difficult. It has been a huge learning curve for me in terms of how to delegate, letting go of control, and developing middle management. So, the whole experience is very strange for me. I am learning a lot here right now so that I don't just stand there and say to the staff 'Why are you doing that? What is going on?' It means that, at some point, I have to let them make their own decisions. It is really hard because these are my places. So, if something goes wrong I believe that it will reflect back on me. At the same time, with all of the people I am developing, they have been loyal and stayed with me for from three to ten years and they probably know how to run the restaurants better than me since I have worked hard to mentor them. When they come to work every day, I want them to feel like I feel when I come to work, energized and excited and happy, so that it doesn't just feel like work."

Restaurant Row

CHICAGO'S CLASSIC RESTAURANT
NEIGHBORHOODS

Rush Street

Although many of Chicago's present-day—and possibly future—classic restaurants would seem to be randomly distributed throughout the city and suburbs, some thoroughfares and neighborhoods were imbued with qualities which, over time, attracted an unusually high concentration of restaurants of a particular ethnicity, style, or trend. In and around Chicago's central area, such places include (in no particular order) Rush Street, Lincoln Park, Streeterville/North Michigan Avenue/Gold Coast, Old Town, River North, the Loop, South Loop, West Loop, Greektown, Taylor Street, and Chinatown.

Beginning in the late '80s and following two decades of stagnation, Rush Street began to be revitalized with upscale hotels and condominiums, high-end boutiques, trendy restaurants with sidewalk cafés, and popular bars. Since opening in 1989 on the site of Mister Kelly's, Gibson has been at the nucleus of Rush Street's renaissance as a popular dining destination. This energetic and charismatic restaurant links Chicago's past penchant for thick, juicy steaks with present-day dining trends. (Eric Bronsky photo).

On the northern fringe of the Rush
Street strip, Newberry Plaza, a residential
building completed in 1974, has been home
to several notable restaurants through
the years. Here, Arnie Morton opened
a sophisticated and imaginative place
called Arnie's. Its three enormous rooms
including the Garden Room and the
main dining room surrounded an atrium;
the $1 million Art Deco motif was as
sumptuous as Arnie's straightforward
American cuisine (Hedrich-Blessing photos,
courtesy of the Chicago History Museum,
HB-38258-A and HB-38258-E).

Other major players who have strived to create new classics here include Phil Stefani Signature Restaurants and Rosebud Restaurants; the latter opened Carmine's in 1994 (Eric Bronsky photo).

Ashkenaz, a classic and revered old-world Jewish style delicatessen in the Rogers Park neighborhood, closed many years ago. In 1990, it was reincarnated as an updated concept around the corner from Rush Street (Eric Bronsky photo).

Rosebud, which began as a Little Italy neighborhood favorite, expanded to other Chicago locations including this former mansion on Rush Street (Eric Bronsky photo).

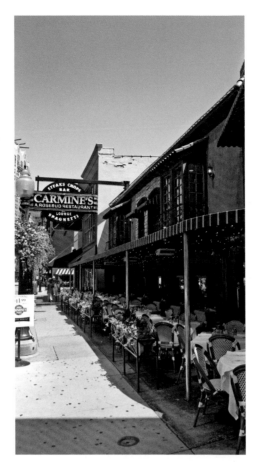

Lincoln Park

Perhaps no other single residential neighborhood in Chicago hosts such a dazzling variety of classic restaurants as the tony Lincoln Park area—from crystal-and-linen elegance to funky and hip—from hamburgers to inventive gastronomy—and with ethnic cuisines from seemingly every corner of the globe in between.

Although buffets where customers could assemble their own salads began appearing in restaurants during the 1950s and '60s, LEYE's R.J. Grunts is credited with enhancing and fine-tuning the concept, thus sending it mainstream. In 1971, unlimited trips to Grunts' "splendrous salad section" (the menu cautioned, "Control yourself!") were included in the price of all dinners. It overflowed not just with greens and toppings, but also an expanded selection of fresh fruits, vegetables, prepared salads, condiments, and soups—around 50 items in all. Grunts' fresh and bountiful salad bar continues to entice diners some 40 years later.

Kevin J. Brown: "Alinea has earned its reputation thanks to Grant Achatz, and the rest of the country correctly rates it near the top of American restaurants. I have only eaten there once, but really enjoyed the experience and think that the food was very good. You also have to look at restaurants like that which have helped garnish Chicago's reputation in the dining industry. I think that we have what is considered by many to be the best restaurant in the country located in Chicago, and that is a big thing. Although New York City has more 'classic' restaurants, I think the best of the best in Chicago are equal to the best of the best in New York City because, in the Midwest, our restaurants have a certain American feel and approachability about them."

LEYE's Gabino Sotelino introduced
Chicago's first Spanish tapas restaurant,
Café Ba-Ba-Reeba!, in 1986

Since 1987, Charlie Trotter's has been
one of the finest restaurants in the country,
earning numerous culinary awards
(Eric Bronsky photos).

Streeterville

*North Michigan
Avenue*

Gold Coast

Eli Schulman posed with his cheesecake that ultimately became one of Chicago's favorite desserts, and also a Taste of Chicago fixture since 1980 (courtesy of Marc Schulman).

As North Michigan Avenue evolved into The Magnificent Mile,® the arrival of new and upscale retail stores and growing pedestrian traffic attracted many restaurateurs to this corridor. Eli's The Place For Steak opened directly opposite the Water Tower Pumping Station in 1966.

An artist-designed menu
for Spiaggia.

The original entrance to
Café Spiaggia (courtesy of
Lawrence Levy).

SPIAGGIA

Kevin J. Brown: "I've always loved and enjoyed the food at Spiaggia. The food created there by Tony Mantuano, and the passion and commitment to the restaurant from Larry Levy, has always been very positive. It has to be on the list of classic restaurants because Spiaggia has stood the test of time and continues to grow. I think that the Signature Room on the 95th floor of the Hancock Center is also a classic in Chicago. The bar located up there is a great place to take friends when they are in town. If you go up there on a fall or spring night, it is just spectacular, and you really get a great picture of the city."

Chef Tony Mantuano, chef/partner, Spiaggia: "I think that the Publican, owned by Paul Kahan and Donnie Madia, is a classic restaurant and will be here for a long time. I love eating there and return to the Publican more than a lot of other restaurants. In addition, the restaurant that has been wildly successful is the Purple Pig, owned by Scott Harris and Jimmy Bannos (I am one of the partners in the restaurant). It has had crazy success and, although open just a year, you would be hard pressed to get a seat in that place. I think that Jimmy's restaurant, Heaven on Seven, is also a classic restaurant. The original one was located in the Garland Building in the Loop, and that place has been around for 50-60 years. It used to be the Garland Building Coffee Shop—a diner—when his dad owned it before he turned it into Heaven on Seven."

Bob Rubin: "We would go to the Consort Room in the Continental Hotel just about every Saturday night, and the owners would always send a bottle of champagne to our table. The food was elegant and the service, fantastic. At that time I was a smoker, and when I would take a cigarette out, there were three hands with lighters in them in front of me ready to light my cigarette. They also had great entertainment there. Each lady would receive a red rose."

Carol Marker: "The Gaslight Club was situated in an old historic home that featured a speakeasy, a library, and French bistro. When you wanted to eat elegant food, there was a small room at the top of the house in kind of an attic with 10-12 tables, beautiful soft music, high-end food, and the maître d' would present each woman with a long stemmed rose. The seating was in very soft, luxurious furniture. You were given a pillow, and then you took your shoes off and put your feet on the pillow. It was a set up for sexy… anything people were thinking about doing afterwards…they had a pretty good chance of it happening."

Chef Jimmy Bannos, Jr.

The Purple Pig opened
in 2010 (courtesy of Restaurant
Intelligence Agency).

River North

Once a seedy urban pocket of dilapidated loft buildings straddling Clark Street's Skid Row, this neighborhood began to attract artists and then evolved into one of Chicago's more compelling restaurant districts. Interspersed among national chains that appeal to tourists are several local classics, including Harry Caray's, Gene and Georgetti, Frontera Grill/ Topolobampo, Kiki's Bistro, and several Lettuce Entertain You restaurants.

Kevin J. Brown: "You have to include Gordon, which was created by Gordon Sinclair, as a classic. He reflected New York style as much as anything which Chicago had. Gordon was stylish, had a wonderful sense of humor in the dining room, brought in great chefs, and had a great eye for the look and style of fine dining. I remember that once, I was working at Shaw's and my wife and I went to Gordon at 11:40 p.m. When we walked in (he knew we were coming), he had made arrangements for us to have a bottle of champagne on ice with two glasses. He was a magnificent host and restaurant owner, and was very proud of his place."

A Gordon's menu cover designed by a local artist (courtesy of Gordon Sinclair).

LEYE opened Scoozi, patterned after a
southern Italian trattoria, in 1986
(Eric Bronsky photo).

Maggiano's Little Italy, begun as a LEYE
concept, has since expanded into a national
chain now owned by Brinker International.
The very first Maggiano's, though, opened
in the River North neighborhood in 1991
(Eric Bronsky photo).

Downtown and 'The Loop'

As Chicagoans and visitors drifted towards hot new neighborhood destinations beginning in the 1960s, classic Loop eateries dwindled to just a handful, including The Berghoff, Miller's Pub, and Italian Village. But Loop revitalization during the1990s and its new identity as a residential community helped to fuel the resurgence of fine dining downtown. In 2001, LEYE opened Petterino's in the heart of the Randolph Street Theatre District. With a 1940s ambience resembling the New York Broadway classic Sardi's, Petterino's was named for the longtime maître d' of The Pump Room (Eric Bronsky photo).

West Loop

Many of Chicago's wholesale food purveyors are located within the Randolph/Fulton Market district. Today, art and photography studios and fine restaurants coexist with the old meat, fish, and produce markets, and an inviting streetscape enhances the gritty industrial area. Randolph Market is also the site of numerous antique, art, and dining festivals (Eric Bronsky photos).

199

Greektown

Susan Herman: "Parthenon is where my husband and I went on our first date, and to this day, Greek food is very special to us. In fact, we always go to a Greek restaurant for our anniversary—not our wedding anniversary, but the anniversary of our first date. The Parthenon back then was a small, two-storefront restaurant in Greektown. You knew the guys who owned it because the guys who were serving you were the guys who owned it. And, we ordered one of everything except calamari—having seen 20,000 Leagues Under The Sea as a kid, I didn't think I was up to dealing with squid and octopus. I also got absolutely polluted on Roditis (a Greek wine)."

Sheila Schlaggar: "A long time ago, we were newly married and we went with another recently married couple to Parthenon. We ordered Roditis. Now, the other girl and I were not necessarily drinkers, but she said it was really good and we kept ordering more. Also, at that time, they did belly dancing up on the tables. So, there was all this music and dancing and we kept drinking the Roditis like it was water—they served it in a jelly jar. When we got up to leave, the other girl was literally on her knees and I could barely stand up. I don't think I ever drank Roditis again. I was lucky that I didn't get sick; I just went to sleep."

Vivo, the first upscale restaurant in the Randolph Street Market area, opened in 1991 (Eric Bronsky photo).

The Parthenon Restaurant, recognized for popularizing gyros and flaming saganaki, is one of several Greektown restaurants within a three-block stretch of South Halsted Street. Other neighborhood classics, including Diana's and Hellas, are fondly recalled (Eric Bronsky photo).

Arnie Weisberg, Sherman Oaks, CA: "A favorite place for me was Diana's in Greektown. I remember there was a grocery store in the front and then about seven or eight tables in the back. It was there that I began eating eggplant with lamb. And there was this wine called Roditis, and when we drank it, it was like drinking water until you tried to stand up. I remember a going-away luncheon for a co-worker that was held at Diana's, and I think we averaged about a bottle of Roditis each. I can still feel the pain."

Judy Robins, Lockport, IL: "The first 'fancy' restaurant that I remember going to—I was in my early 20s and dating a man who was a resident at Cook County Hospital—he took me to the Greek Islands in Greektown. This was the old location before they moved across the street. It was the very first time I saw a belly dancer and my eyes popped out of my head. She danced around our table, and people put money in her belt. In the '80s we had an art gallery that was right behind the restaurant, so often, after the gallery would close, we would go over there. Mike, the owner, whose wife was also an artist, liked us a lot and he would feed us Ouzo. And of course, we would get drunk and rowdy. I still go there often."

Phil Shapiro: "I got knocked out cold at Hellas—I was home from the Marine Corps and a bunch of us went to Hellas to eat. We were drinking Ouzo and they had entertainment there—a belly dancer. Well, she was up on the stage and she started pointing her finger at me, and I thought she was giving me a 'come-on.' So, I got up on the stage with her and I was dancing and I'm in uniform. She started playing with the buckle on my pants, so I just undid the buckle and dropped my pants. What I didn't know was that the bongo drummer was her husband. Of course, I was drunk, and the next thing I knew, I was feeling this searing pain as he broke a bottle on my head. They carried me out of there."

Suburbs

There are, of course, many restaurants of note well beyond Chicago's core. Suburban 'restaurant rows' are practically ubiquitous, and clusters of eateries typically surround regional shopping malls. But these are almost always formulaic national chains and franchises rather than local classics. There are some groupings of classic eateries, though, along such arteries as Sheridan Road through Highwood or Milwaukee Avenue through Wheeling—the latter was anchored by Le Francais for many years. It should be noted that some of today's suburban eateries, (e.g. the Francesca restaurants), are actually outposts of the original Chicago classics.

A couple of Wheeling's most revered classics closed in recent years—Le Francais and the last of Don Roth's Blackhawk restaurants. But since opening in 1982, Bob Chinn's Crab House has been wildly successful, expanding to over 700 seats, and currently the fourth top-grossing independent restaurant in the country. Chicago's legendary Superdawg opened its first suburban location right next door to Chinn's. An outpost of Phil Stefani's Tuscany is thriving just down the street (Eric Bronsky photo).

Bob Kregas, Hillside, IL: "My wife and I got married in 1971, and we moved to Melrose Park. There was a restaurant starting up called The Millionaires Club, where you had to purchase a membership and back then—I'm talking 1972-73—the membership was like 30 or 40 dollars. The place was started by Chris Carson, who eventually opened Carson's Ribs and then Boston Blackie's Restaurants. All the drinks were free, so if you went there for dinner and you were a drinker, you could get pretty well lit for free. The catch was, it was cheap booze. I used to order the pork chops, which were like $18.95. Remember, this was the early '70s, so you were paying for your drinks through the price of your dinner. But, it was just cool to have a membership card in The Millionaires Club and go there for dinner. The food was good, but it wasn't great. It was an edgy place, nonetheless."

Interviewee Index